A MULTIFACETED JEWEL

Studies On The Local Church

About the author

Boon-Sing Poh was born in Malaysia in 1954. Brought up in a pagan background, he was saved by God's grace through faith in Jesus Christ while studying in the United Kingdom. He returned to Malaysia to become a lecturer in a university for six years, founded the first Reformed Baptist Church in the country in 1983, and was imprisoned for his faith from 1987 to 1988 for a period of 325 days. He is the pastor of Damansara Reformed Baptist Church (DRBC) in Kuala Lumpur, a contented husband, a thankful father of four sons, and a happy grandfather. He earned the PhD degree in Electronics Engineering from the University of Liverpool, UK, the Diploma in Religious Study from Cambridge University, UK, and the PhD degree in Theology from North-West University, SA.

A MULTIFACETED JEWEL

Studies On The Local Church

BOON-SING POH

Published by

Good News Enterprise

A MULTIFACETED JEWEL: Studies On The Local Church

Published by:

GOOD NEWS ENTERPRISE, 52 Jalan SS 21/2,

Damansara Utama, 47400 Petaling Jaya, Malaysia.

www.rbcm.net; www.ghmag.net

Printed by:

Kindle Direct Publishing, an Amazon company, United States of America. Typeset by the author using TeXworks, the memoir class.

This book is dedicated to

the members of

Damansara Reformed Baptist Church.

Contents

Contents

PREFACE TO THIS EDITION

The substance of this book remains largely the same as the original version, except for minor tweaks in a few places. It has been used to prepare prospective members for constituting into churches in pioneering situations. It has been taught also to our congregations once every few years. Ignorance of the privileges, responsibilities, and liabilities of church membership is a cause of many churches remaining weak. The quality is more important than the number of the churches we plant. It is hoped that this book will be appreciated by more churches, both in pioneering as well as the more established situations.

Boon-Sing Poh,
Kuala Lumpur, May 2020.

PREFACE

The local church is a multifaceted jewel. It is the body of Christ, bought by His blood and cleansed by His word. While it is impossible to find a perfect church in this world, each local church should strive to be as closely conformed to the biblical ideal as possible. This is a task that church leaders will want to be engaged in, and church members will want to know more about.

This book explains, in short chapters, the various facets of the life of a biblical church. It is particularly suitable for pioneering situations in which believers are being prepared for covenanting together as churches. The new, as well as older, believers will be helped to have a clearer understanding of the local church.

The title of each chapter is followed by one or two Bible references, which should be read as the background to the topic under study. The proof-texts in the chapter may be ignored without affecting the flow of thought, although the serious student would want to check them up. Those who are leading others in the study of this book should check them out in advance.

The substance of this book has largely been culled from other sources, chief of which is "Local Church Practice", by Baruch Maoz et. al. (Carey Publications, 1978). It has evolved to its present form after having been used to found, and establish, a number of new churches in Malaysia. It is our hope and prayer that this book will be helpful to many others elsewhere.

Boon-Sing Poh,
Kuala Lumpur, 1997.

One

CENTRAL AND UNIQUE (Acts 2:40-47)

We wish to show that the local church is central and unique in the purposes of God. *Central*, meaning that it plays an important part, it is the focal point, in the outworking of God's purposes. *Unique*, meaning that it is special, one of its kind, with no possibility of replacement.

Before that, we must be clear what a local church is. Wrong ideas of the church prevail:

i There are those who think that it is the building in which Christians meet. This has caused people to want bigger, nicer, and more of such "churches".

ii In reaction to that wrong idea, others have emphasised that it is not the building but the people who gather to worship. However, that is only partially true. Those who hold to this view tend to downplay the importance of a properly constituted church, and claim that it is good enough for them to meet casually with other believers, say, at their place of work. They also are in favour of Christians forming various "para-church organisations", i.e. organisations that exist alongside local churches.

We believe that the Bible is the only authority in all matters of doctrine and practice. What does it teach about the church? Let us find out, and let us follow its teaching!

1.1   What Is A Church?

1 The Greek word *ekklesia* is used 115 times in the New Testament. The word means "a called out group of people". It can refer to any gathering of people, regardless of whether they are Christians or not. It is therefore translated as "church" or "assembly" in the Bible. In reference to the Christian assembly, it is used in only two ways:

(i) All true believers considered together, whether past, present, or future. This is the "universal church" e.g. Ephesians 5:25, 27; Matthew 16:18.

(ii) Disciples of Jesus Christ gathered in a particular locality. This is the "local church", e.g. Acts 20:17; 1 Corinthians 1:2; Revelation 1:11; 2:1. *Ekklesia* is used more than 90 times in this sense.

2 The universal church is *invisible* in the sense that the work of the Holy Spirit in the lives of believers cannot be seen. We, therefore, do not know exactly who, or how many, are in the invisible church. Attempts to define a 'visible' universal church, based on Acts 9:31, Acts 15, and Matthew 13 are unconvincing.[1]

---

[1]The argument is that the word "church" is singular in Acts 9:31, showing that the various congregations in Judea, Galilee and Samaria together formed a "denomination" or a "visible universal church". We believe, however, that the plural,

3 The universal church manifests itself as *visible* local churches in the world. Believers may be recognised by a credible profession of faith. From Acts 2:40-47, and related passages such as 2 Corinthians 6:16-18 and Hebrews 8:7-13, we learn that the local church possesses the following marks:

(i) It is made up of baptised believers;

(ii) They voluntarily associate together under special covenant;

(iii) They maintain worship, the truths, the ordinances, and the discipline of the gospel.

Definition: "A local church is a congregation of believers in Christ, baptised on credible profession of faith, and voluntarily associated under special covenant for the maintenance of the worship, the truths, the ordinances, and the discipline, of the gospel" (Harvey, 1982).[2]

4 Membership in a local church does not always coincide with membership in the universal church, and vice versa. Professed believers who are unregenerate may be unwittingly admitted into the

---

"churches", is correct because that is found in the more reliable Received Text, which is the manuscript used in translating the King James and the New King James versions of the Bible. Moreover, the plural is used in every passage where congregations in a region are referred to, e.g. Galatians 1:2; 2 Corinthians 8:1; Revelation 1:11. Furthermore, it is precarious to build a doctrine on a controversial verse.

In Acts 15, only two churches were involved in the so-called Council of Jerusalem, namely the church of Antioch and that of Jerusalem. No delegate was sent by any of the churches that Paul and Barnabas visited en route (v. 3). The gathering of the representatives of Antioch and Jerusalem is not called another "church", as the Presbyterians would like us to believe (cf. v. 22).

In Matthew 13, the parable of the wheat and the tares is not the description of a "visible universal church" made up of believers and non-believers. Rather, it is explained that the field (v. 24) is the world (v. 38).

[2]The church covenant is discussed in chapter 12 of this book. Keach's Catechism, which was widely used by the Particular Baptists of the seventeenth century, contains a definition of the visible church and the invisible church. These are missing in the Shorter Catechism, produced by the Westminster Assembly, which was basically Presbyterian.

membership of the local church, as was the case with Ananias and Sapphira (Acts 5). Also, true believers may be precluded, by circumstances or through ignorance, from membership with a local congregation for a time, as was the case with the Ethiopian eunuch (Acts 8). These practical implications follow:

(i) You are not necessarily a member of the universal church simply because you are a member of a local church. In other words, you may not be converted yet!

(ii) If you are a member of the invisible universal church by regeneration (i.e. being born again by the Holy Spirit), you ought to become a member of a local church through water baptism.

1.2   Central And Unique

1 The local church plays an important part in the outworking of God's plan.

(i) The formation of local churches, by the calling out of the elect from all over the world, was anticipated in the Old Testament, e.g. Isaiah 2:3; 56:6-7; Jeremiah 31:31-34. There will be the gathering in of believers from all nations. They will worship God in various churches, in which God's word is proclaimed (Eccl. 12:11).

(ii) The Lord anticipated it in His ministry on earth (Matt. 18:15-17). The final court of appeal in disciplinary cases is "the church" which, at that time, consisted of the apostles. The apostles represented the local churches that were to be formed later.

(iii) The apostles understood the Great Commission as involving the planting of local churches (Matt. 28:18-20; Acts 1:7-8; 13:1ff.; 14:23).

(iv) The vision of the lampstands, in Revelation 1-3, confirms that it is God's plan to have local churches till Christ returns.

2 Christ's glory is to be seen in the universal church (Eph. 3:21). In practice, this means local churches (2 Cor. 6:16; Eph. 2:19-22; Rev. 1:13). That is why it is a serious thing when a church compromises with the world and becomes unfaithful to the Lord.

3 It is the local church that is the pillar and ground of the truth; not individuals, not denominations, not national churches, not para-church organisations (1 Tim. 3:15). It is the pillar that holds up the gospel so that its light shines in the world. It is the foundation on which the faith of believers are built up.

4 The epistles of the New Testament were written almost exclusively to churches or individuals associated with churches.

5 The Scripture relates all gospel work to churches:

(i) Paul was a member of the church at Antioch (Acts 11:26), was sent out by that church (Acts 13:2-3), and returned to render an account (Acts 14:26-28). The same happened in the second missionary journey, and also in the third, when he was arrested before arriving back at Antioch (Acts 15:35-36; 18:19-22; 18:23).

(ii) Timothy was incorporated into the missionary team from the local church of Lystra (Acts 16:1ff.).

(iii) Preachers are to be sent out by the local church (Matt. 9:38; 28:19; Acts 13:1-3; Rom. 10:15).

6 The Scripture relates the lives of believers to the churches:

(i) Believers should worship with other believers in church (Heb. 10:25; Acts 2:46-47; 20:7; Psalm 84).

(ii) The church is the place where believers get oversight over their souls (Heb. 13:7,17).

(iii) The church is the place where believers get teaching, training and correction (2 Tim. 3:16-4:2; Tit. 2).

(iv) The "means of grace" are found in the church: fellowship, hearing God's word preached, baptism, the Lord's Supper, etc. (1 Cor. 11:23-26).

1.3   Some Important Conclusions

1 All gospel work should issue out of the local church, be subservient to its discipline, and be supported by its prayers and blessing. It is unbiblical for individuals to go about doing their own work in God's name, and be answerable to nobody (cf. Acts 9:20, 27).

2 There is no biblical basis for modern-day missionary societies and para-church organisations. Specific gospel activities that are unable to be carried out by individual churches may be carried out by a group of churches which are in fellowship with one another (Acts 11:22-26; 16:1-3; 1 Cor. 16:1-3; Rom. 15:26; Phil. 4:10-17; etc.). Missionary societies formed by churches fall into this category. How closely such gospel work is to be supervised by the churches will depend on the nature of the work and the people involved. Generally speaking, those approved or assigned by the chur-ches to some gospel work should be given the liberty to act according to their discretion.

3 If you have a "high view" of the local church, you would:

(i) Commit yourself as a member to a good local church. Note that it might be necessary for you to separate from an apostate church (2 Cor. 6:17; 2 Thess. 3:6, 14-15; etc.).

(ii) Order your life around the local church. Family, career, recreation, etc., should be organised to revolve around the local church.

(iii) Aim to build up the local church. There is no better way to glorify God than to serve Him by building up faithful churches.

Questions

1 Evangelists or missionaries should be people sent out by local churches. Does that mean Christians should not actively spread the gospel?

2 A student finds that all his spare time is taken up by Christian Union activities at university. He finds it hard even to go for worship in church on Sundays. What can you say about him?

3 The term "local church" speaks of "location" (where a church is located) and "locality" (catering for the people in an area). Need a believer be a member of the church nearest his home? How far away should the church be from him? What factors should determine the choice of which church to join? Take into consideration the good roads and improved transportation today. Does a pioneering situation make any difference?

Reference

1 Harvey, Hezekiah. 1982. The Church: Its Polity and Ordinances. Backus.

Two

DOCTRINE (2 Tim. 3:16-4:5)

Acts 2:42 tells us that the early church "continued steadfastly in the apostles' doctrine and fellowship, in the breaking of bread, and in prayers." Clearly, doctrine occupied an important place in the life of the church. The "apostles' doctrine" is mentioned first.

What is "the apostles' doctrine"? We know that it is the teaching of the whole Bible, from the following considerations:

i We know that the apostles considered the Old Testament to be the word of God, just as the Lord Jesus Christ did.

ii We know that the Lord caused the New Testament to be written down as the revelation of God (John 16:12-15). The apostles knew that what they were teaching and writing were actually the word of God (1 Thess. 2:13; 2 Pet. 3:15-16).

iii The Bible itself declares that "all Scripture is given by inspiration of God (2 Tim. 3:16-17)." The "all Scripture", at that time, included at least the Old Testament (v. 15), Paul's own teachings (2 Tim. 3:14 cf. v. 10, 1:13, and 2:2), the teachings of all the other apostles (2 Pet. 3:15-16; Eph. 2:20), and Matthew's gospel (1 Tim. 5:18 cf. Matt. 10:10).

The Bible alone is our authority in all matters of faith and practice. Doctrine in and of itself is useless. The purpose of doctrine is to reveal God, save souls, and change lives (Gal. 3:22-25; Rom. 10:17; 2 Pet. 3:18). Doctrine comes first, practice follows.

How should the importance of doctrine show itself in the church? It is shown in at least two ways: by having a Confession of Faith, and by the public instruction of the word.

2.1   The Importance Of The Confession Of Faith

1 A doctrinal standard for the church is essential:

(i) *To preserve and uphold the truth.* Every church claims to believe in the Bible. Yet, there are differences in belief and practice. Our church distinctives are known and preserved by a Confession of Faith. A Statement of Faith is useful, but too scanty. It is only a "statement", giving a few points of beliefs that show that we are a true church. Some churches have Statements of Faith which we can agree with but they may also hold to other teachings, not mentioned in their Statements of Faith, which we cannot agree with!

(ii) *To expose, counter, and exclude errors and heresies.* Wrong teachings tend to reappear. How are we to uphold the truth without knowing what the truth is? How are we to exclude, say, a Jehovah's Witness from the membership of the church? He may believe that Jesus Christ is the Son of God, but he does not believe that He is God!

2 Some important points must be noted:

(i) To have a clearly defined body of truth is not a concept that is foreign to the Bible. The Bible speaks of "the apostles' doctrine" (Acts 2:42); "the doctrine which you learned" (Rom. 16:17); "the gospel that you received" (Gal. 1:6-9; 1 Cor. 15:1); "the faith which was once for all delivered to the saints" (Jude 3); "the things which you heard... commit to faithful men..." (2 Tim. 2:2); "holding fast the faithful word" (Tit. 1:9); "the tradition... received from us" (2 Thess. 3:6). The early Christians knew that there was this body of truth, called "the faith" (Jude 3), that had been preserved for God's people. In contrast, many Christians today are so vague about what they believe in.

(ii) If we dare to proclaim truths by mouth, we should dare to put down those truths in writing as well. When our beliefs are written down systematically, we have effectively a Confession of Faith! We do not wish to "re-invent the wheel", however. We adopt the 1689 Baptist Confession of Faith as the doctrinal standard of our church. Other Reformed churches hold to one or the other of the Confessions of Faith that arose from the Reformation. The 1689 Baptist Confession of Faith is the most well-developed of all the historic Confessions of Faith. It builds upon the earlier Confessions of Faith, correcting and improving upon them. It teaches believer's baptism, and upholds Independency as the biblical form of church government.

(iii) We do not treat the Confession of Faith as an authority equal to Scripture. It merely contains the important truths which we believe to be biblical, and are laid down systematically, in a form that is convenient for easy reference.

(iv) The Bible does allow for differences of opinion on non-fundamental matters (1 Cor. 11:19 cf. 1:10; Phil. 3:15 cf. 2:1-4).

It *permits* differences on such matters, but it does not *approve* of such differences. It expects all believers to come to agreement on more and more matters as they mature. In the church, you may act according to your understanding of truth as long as that does not give rise to division (Rom. 16:17), and as long as you hold to the fundamental beliefs laid down in the Confession of Faith.

(v) Preserving our doctrinal distinctives has not in any way hindered our fellowship with other true churches of Christ. It has, in fact, helped us to determine who we may fellowship with, and to what extent. A lot of people today talk about unity between churches but forget that true unity can exist only around the truth. There is no merit in being loose, shallow, and compromising over doctrine.

2.2 The Importance Of The Public Instruction Of The Word

1 The Bible has a lot to say about preaching and teaching, directed at believers and non-believers. It will help if we are clear about three basic words used to describe these activities.

(i) The word "preaching" is derived from the Greek *kerusso*, to proclaim, herald, announce with authority (Matt. 11:1; 1 Cor. 1:21, 23; 2:4; 15:14; 1 Tim. 2:7; 2 Tim. 1:11; Acts 20:26). The word "teaching" is derived from the Greek word *didasko*, to teach, instruct (Matt. 11:1; 1 Tim 2:11). There is considerable overlap between the two. In both, doctrines and instructions are imparted, illustrations are used, implications are spelt out. That is why, in 1 Timothy 2:7, 2 Timothy 1:11, Colossians 1:28, and Acts 28:31, "teaching" is explanatory of "preaching". Often, the word "teaching" is used as a general term covering all the other activities of imparting knowledge (e.g. 1 Tim. 3:2; 4:11; 6:3; 1 Cor. 12:28, 29; James 3:1).

(ii) There are also differences between preaching and teaching: in the substance, manner of delivery, occasion or circumstances, and effects (Rom. 12:7, 8; 1 Cor. 2:4; etc.). Preaching deals more with application, teaching more with doctrine; preaching is hortatory (exhortational, to make you act), teaching is didactic (for instruction, to make you know); preaching is formal, public, and directed to a diverse crowd, while teaching is informal, private, and directed to a homogeneous group. Preaching searches the conscience, stirs the heart, and moves one to action. Teaching removes ignorance, corrects errors, and informs the mind.[1] The difference is like that between a politician addressing a large crowd and a lecturer teaching in a lecture theatre. This difference is brought out in passages like Matthew 11:1, where Jesus "departed from there *to teach and to preach* in their cities."

(iii) The phrase "to preach the gospel" is a translation of the Greek word *euangelizomai* (Acts 8:4; 1 Cor. 1:17). It means to publish, or bring, the good news to others. It is best translated as to "evangelise". This includes the activities of preaching (Rom. 10:14-17; Acts 10:42; 20:25), teaching (Acts 18:11; 28:31; 1 Tim. 2:7; 2 Tim. 1:11), disputing (Acts 9:28), reasoning (Acts 17:2, 17; 18:4; 19:9); persuading (Acts 18:4; 19:8, 26; 28:23); etc.

Our concern here is more with preaching and teaching in the church.

2 The Bible places great importance on the public preaching of God's

---

[1] 1 This was also the view of the Puritans. See, for example, Thomas Goodwin, Works, Vol. 11, pp. 336, 337, 502, 503.

word.

(i) The Old Testament prophets were preachers, e.g. Jeremiah, Amos, Hosea, Isaiah, etc. Similarly the New Testament characters, e.g. the Lord Jesus Christ, John the Baptist, Paul, Peter, etc.

(ii) There is constant emphasis on the need to preach: (a) to save souls (Rom. 10:13-17; 1 Pet. 1:23); (b) to build up believers (Eph. 4:11ff.; Tit. 2:1ff; 1 Tim. 4:6, 11-16); (c) to uphold the truth (2 Tim. 2:2, 15, 24; 2 Tim. 4:1-5).

(iii) There is constant emphasis on hearing (Matt. 11:15; 13:9; Mark 4:9, 23-24).

(iv) The primary duty of the church, and the preacher, is to preach the word of God, and not to do social work or be involved in politics (Acts 6:1-4; 2 Tim. 3:16-17 cf. 4:1-4).

3 Apart from public preaching, there should be private teaching in which there is opportunity for discussion and answering of questions. Ideally, the church members should be taught together, apart from the mixed crowd in the worship service (cf. 1 Cor. 14:23-25). But circumstances may require that particular groups be ministered to separately, e.g. housewives with young children who are unable to attend the week-night meetings, doctors and nurses who are unable to attend the regular meetings because of shift duties. The Lord engaged in teaching (Matt. 13:36; 16:13; 18:1; 21:20; 24:1, 3; etc.). The apostles also engaged in teaching (Acts 19:9; 20:20; 28:23, 31). Note that even in teaching, doctrines and instructions are *given*, and *with authority* (Acts 20:7, 9; 1 Tim. 4:6, 11; 2 Tim. 4:2; Tit. 2:15). Why then the clamour today for the "discussion-and-dialogue" type of Bible study?

2.3 Doctrine And You

1 Do not despise doctrine. Make every effort to increase your understanding of the Bible's teaching by: hearing, reading, studying, meditating, memorising, discussing. Truths come "line by line, precept by precept" (Isa. 28:9-14). How is your attendance at preaching and teaching sessions?

2 Does your church uphold the importance of doctrine? If it does, the preaching of God's word will be central in the worship service – not the Lord's Supper, not music and singing, not entertainment, not testimonies, not healing, not story-telling. And why not introduce the 1689 Confession of Faith into your church?

3 Be proud, in the right sense, to be associated with a doctrinal church. Live up to the doctrines we believe in, so that no one can say anything against us (2 Pet. 3:18). Pray for the preacher, that he might remain faithful to God's word and not be discouraged by opposition. Prepare your hearts to hear preaching, concentrate when hearing, and retain what you hear.

Questions

1 How would you answer a person who says that:

(i) He only believes in the Bible and does not need a man-made creed like the 1689 Confession of Faith?

(ii) He reads only the Bible and would not read books written by men?

(iii) He believes that conduct is more important than doctrine?

2 Compare the advantages and disadvantages of Bible studies that are conducted in a "teaching" style and in a "discussion-and-dialogue"

style. The latter has been called "interactive Bible Study". How accurate is that description?

3 Why do you think Christians and churches are so opposed to doctrine and to Confessions of Faith? How true are these reasons? What can we do to change the situation?

Reference

1 Goodwin, Thomas. Works, Vol. 11. Banner of Truth Trust.

Three

FELLOWSHIP (Eph. 4:1-16)

Fellowship is one of the marks of the New Testament church (Acts 2:42). It is not the only mark. Do not think a church good simply because it seems to have warm fellowship. Equally, it is not to be a missing mark. A church that is strong on doctrine, but weak in fellowship, is defective. Its importance becomes clear as we understand its essence and its relevance to the life of the church.

3.1   The Basis Of Fellowship

1 Fellowship (Greek, *koinonia*) is derived from *koinos*, meaning common. To have fellowship is to have things in common, to share, to participate together, to be in partnership. Christian fellowship is spiritual in nature, expressing itself in life. It is not merely sharing the things we have, but the sharing of our own selves. We share a common spiritual life.

2 Our fellowship with other Christians and other churches depends to a great extent upon three factors:

(i) *Spiritual life.* There is no fellowship between light and darkness, between a believer and a non-believer (2 Cor. 6:14-16). Friendship is not to be confused with fellowship. There may be warmth and acceptance between two good friends, but that is different from fellowship. Fellowship exists only between those who have spiritual life, i.e. those who have faith in Christ, who are indwelt by the Holy Spirit (1 Jn. 1:3,7; 1 Cor. 6:19-20).

(ii) *Truth.* Fellowship is based on truth. Those who have spiritual life are drawn to truth (1 Jn. 1:5-7; Jn. 3:20-21). The more of truth we share in common, the stronger is the fellowship, and vice versa (Eph. 4:1-6).

(iii) *Obedience.* Belief is one thing, obedience another. There is constant emphasis on obedience to the truth in the Bible (1 Jn. 2:3-5; Jn. 14:15, 21, 23, 24). Fellowship is grievously broken when one party acts contrary to professed truth. C. H. Spurgeon was heart-broken by those who acted contrary to their professed beliefs during the "Downgrade Controversy".

3 Fellowship is closely connected with unity. The following may be said about unity:

(i) *Spiritual unity is created by God, not by man.* In essence and in principle, unity already exists between Christians. We do not strive to *create* unity. We strive to *maintain* (Eph. 4:1-6), and *express* (Jn. 17:20-23), that unity.

(ii) *This unity is to be manifested primarily in the local church,* and then between believers at large. This arises from the fact that the universal church manifests itself in the world primarily in the form of local churches (Jn. 17:20-23 cf. Matt. 18:17; Eph. 3:10, 21; Rev. 1:9-20) In the church, love is to be expressed. Love is both a gift and a responsibility. As a gift, it comes from God. As a responsibility, we must exert effort to show it (1 Cor. 13).

(iii) *Selective fellowship is necessary* because of three reasons.

Firstly, it is taught in the Bible. Positively speaking, we are to do good to everyone, but especially to the household of faith (Gal. 6:10). Negatively speaking, we must separate from those who depart from fundamental truths, whether in doctrine or in practice. There are those whom we must continue to regard as brothers (2 Thess. 3:6, 14-15). There are others whom we must regard as unbelievers, and even enemies of the gospel (Matt. 18:17; 2 Cor. 6:14-18; Rom. 16:17; Gal. 1:8-9; 2 Jn. 7-11).

Secondly, we have the example of the Lord in his dealings with the disciples. From all those who followed Him, He chose only seventy to send out two by two. From the seventy, He chose only twelve to be apostles. Among the twelve were three – namely, Peter, James and John – who accompanied Him to the Mount of Transfiguration and the Garden of Gethsamane. Among the three was one known as "the disciple whom the Lord loved".

Thirdly, there is the consideration that in practice it is impossible to fellowship with everyone equally. Our time and resources are limited. Interests, personalities, and circumstances differ. Moreover, there are different degrees of understanding of, and obedience to, truths among God's people.

4 From all we have learned – the centrality and uniqueness of the local church, the importance of doctrine, the expression of unity between Christians – the following principle emerges: *The local church should be doctrinally and socially one* (1 Cor. 1:10; Phil. 3:16; 4:2; 1 Cor. 12:12; Eph. 4:1-6). This calls for:

(i) An agreed system of belief, and hence the Confession of Faith.

(ii) The whole church to be gathered together as one, as far as possible. We deliberately avoid fragmentation into groups: cell-groups, women's fellowship; youth fellowship, etc. However, there is a place for specialised witness (cf. Gal. 2:7-9). For example, there may be a women's fellowship or a youth fellowship geared towards bringing the gospel to women and youths, respectively.

(iii) A recognition that it is impossible for every member to know all others equally well. Acceptance of this fact will prevent criticism of the fellowship in the church. It will also help us to avoid having romantic ideas of fellowship: living in communes, erasing all ideas of private property, having joy all the time, etc. Effort is needed to know everyone better, especially when the church grows bigger. Christians must "grow in the grace and knowledge of the Lord and Saviour Jesus Christ" (2 Pet. 3:18). The church must grow to become glorious, "not having spot or wrinkle or any such thing, but that it should be holy and without blemish" (Eph. 5:27). We may not know everyone in the church equally well, but the fellowship between the members must always be growing.

3.2   How Fellowship Expresses Itself

We consider the practical ways by which fellowship should be expressed.

1 *Around worship, teaching and prayer* (Acts 2:1, 42; 4:23; 20:7; Col. 4:16; Heb. 10:25; 1 Cor. 16:2).

(i) Many are those who complain of the lack of fellowship and yet do not attend the public meetings of the church. Effort should be made to attend all the meetings of the church. Every time a member is absent, he is missed. How can it be otherwise? We are a fellowship, a church made up of members who have covenanted together. A brother or sister who does not come home for the Chinese New Year reunion dinner is sorely missed. A closely knitted church will miss a member who does not turn up for a meeting.

(ii) We want to come prepared, and ready to participate. By participation we do not mean that everyone should be contributing an item. This wrong understanding of participation is taught in many churches. It arises from a wrong understanding of 1 Corinthians 14:26. What we mean is that our hearts must be in what we are doing corporately (cf. Matt. 15:8; 1 Cor. 14:16). When someone leads the church in prayer, our hearts must be in what he is praying. When we listen together, and sing together, our hearts must be in what we are doing.

(iii) As a church, we keep public meetings to a minimum, but we expect attendance at the maximum. It would be good if there is spontaneous desire to meet around the word and for prayer everyday of the week (cf. Acts 2:46). In practice, this is not possible. That's why most churches have special time off together, once or twice a year – in retreats, church camps, or conferences. As far as the church meetings are concerned, we keep to the rule of "minimum meetings, maximum attendance".

2 *In Christian service, including evangelism and good works.*

(i) The Lord organised evangelism, sending out His disciples two by two to preach. The members of the early church were engaged in spreading the gospel everywhere. The church today should be actively engaged in evangelism.

(ii) Then, there is good works to be done. The sick need to be visited. The old and infirmed need to be ministered to. There is much scope for visitation of hospitals, prisons, drug rehabilitation centres and refugee camps (Gal. 6:10; James 1:27).

3 *In hospitality and social interaction around a meal* (Acts 2:46; 1 Cor. 11:21-22; 1 Pet. 4:9).

(i) Sharing a meal speaks of mutual acceptance and unity (cf. 1 Cor. 10:16-17, 18, 19-21; Rev. 3:20; 19:9). When was the last time you invited someone home for a meal? The families in the church should invite one another for a meal. They should also invite the single people in the church. This is an important ministry that will go a long way to promote fellowship. This need not be done every week. But an attempt should be made to do so on a regular basis, perhaps once in a month or in two months.

(ii) There is also a place for fellowship-meals that are organised for the whole church (Acts 2:46; 1 Cor. 11:21-22; Rev. 19:9). Whether it is held once a month or once in three months, church members should see that this is a part of the church's life and attempt to attend.

(iii) Hospitality extended to non-Christian friends together with church members form an effective bridge in witnessing. When there are no conversions in the church for a long stretch of time, it may be due to the fact that non-Christian friends have not been invited home for meals. We must pray for conversions. We must evangelise. But we must also befriend our contacts in a genuine way and expose them to Christian values and warmth seen over a meal.

(iv) We are expected to share only what we have, and no more. You are not required to cook expensive dishes. For example, *bee-hoon* (noodles) fried in soya-sauce, with eggs and bean sprouts, make a wholesome meal that is not at all expensive!

(v) We must learn the grace of accepting, not just giving. There are certain individuals who always turn down invitations to a meal. Such people not only lose out because they are not edified, but also because they are unable to edify others.

4 *In informal, private fellowship.*

(i) Regular visits should be encouraged, in which there is mutual edification through:

> (a) What we say: to encourage, instruct, reprove, pray, share our experiences (Eph. 4:29; 2 Tim. 1:16-18; Acts 18:24-28; James 5:16; Rom. 12:9-12).

> (b) What we do: sharing burdens, finance, possession, etc. (Gal. 6:2; Acts 2:44-45; 4:32-37; Rom. 12:13;1 Pet. 5:10-11).

(ii) Christians can legitimately have an interest in all spheres of life, as long as they are subjected to Christ's lordship: art, literature, music, sports, etc. (Ps. 24:1). If possible, carry out such interests together, e.g. outings, games for children, cooking, etc.

3.3   Conclusion

Fellowship in the church should be a reflection of the fellowship that we are going to have in heaven. While on earth, there is much that spoils our fellowship: trials and tribulations, toils and tears, strife and misunderstandings, and sin. We must, nevertheless, strive to improve on our fellowship so that we may be prepared for the perfect fellowship of heaven.

> Behold, how good and how pleasant it is For brethren to dwell together in unity! It is like the precious oil upon the

head, Running down on the beard, The beard of Aaron, Running down on the edge of his garments, It is like the dew of Hermon, Descending upon the mountains of Zion; For there the Lord commanded the blessing -Life forevermore. (Psalm 133)

Questions

1 Suggest some practical ways of improving and encouraging fellowship in our church.

2 Hebrews 13:2 encourages us to entertain strangers. Does this pose any problem to us? (Cf. Gal. 6:10.)

3 Many modern churches have "cell groups". Shouldn't we have them as well? What principles and factors should govern our decision? Consider the value of having scattered groups meeting separately with outreach as its main purpose.

Four

BAPTISM (Acts 8:26-40)

Baptism is one of two *special ordinances* instituted by our Lord, the other being the Lord's Supper. There are other ordinances, or "means of grace", such as the word of God and prayer. "Baptism and the Lord's Supper differ from the other ordinances of God in that they were specially instituted by Christ to represent and apply to believers the benefits of the new covenant by visible and outward signs" (Keach's Catechism, Q. 99).

The Roman Catholic Church teaches that there are seven "sacraments", viz. baptism, confirmation (i.e. the laying on of hands to convey the Holy Spirit), eucharist (i.e. the mass), penance (i.e. the forgiving of sins by priests), extreme unction (i.e. special prayer and the anointing of oil upon the sick), marriage, and orders (i.e. the ordination of priests and consecration of nuns). It is claimed that, apart from marriage and orders, which are optional, the other sacraments are indispensable to salvation. In view of this perversion of the word "sacrament" (*an oath*, Latin), we prefer to use the word "ordinance" (*an authoritative direction*). The 1689 Confession (Chapters 28-30) as well as Keach's Catechism (Questions 99, 100 & 107) use the word "ordinance".

From after the time of the apostles, there have been two types of churches: the "establishment churches" and the "dissenting churches". One chief difference between the two is on baptism: the dissenting churches practise only believer's baptism, while the establishment churches practise infant baptism as well. This long-standing differ-ence should not cause us to despair over the situation. Instead, we should come to a clear biblical position because:

  i We believe that the Bible is authoritative, sufficient and perspic-uous (i.e. may be clearly understood).

 ii Baptism is such a prominent feature of New Testament leaching that it is impossible for us to remain unclear about it. Direct teachings, examples, allusions, and figurative uses, of baptism are given. Together, the noun "baptism" (*baptisma*) and the verb "to baptise" (*baptizo*) occur about a hundred time Both words come from *bapto*, to dip. *Baptisma* must not b confused with *baptismos*, which is a reference to ceremonil washing of articles (Heb. 6:2, 9:10; Mark 7:4, 8). *Baptizo* must not be confused with *rhantizo*, to sprinkle (Heb. 9:13; 10:22).

iii The controversy through the centuries would have exhausted the main arguments on both sides so that we are now in a position to consider which is right and which is wrong.

4.1   The Meaning And Purpose

Baptism has both a meaning and a purpose.[1]

---

[1]The difference between "meaning" and "purpose" should be noted. If I were to take out my pen from the pocket, you might ask me, "What is the purpose of taking out the pen?" You would not ask me, "What is the meaning of taking out

1 *Meaning:* It is a sign of –

(i) fellowship with Christ in His death, burial and resurrection (Rom. 6:3-4; Col. 2:12);

(ii) spiritual union with Christ (Gal. 3:26-27);

(iii) remission of sins (Acts 22:16; 1 Pet. 3:21; Mark 16:16);

(iv) separation from the world to walk in newness of life with Christ (Rom. 6:3-4; 1 Pet. 3:18-22).

2 *Purpose:* Initiation into the family of God, i.e. the local church (Acts 2:41; John 3:3, 5; 1 Cor. 12:13; Gal. 3:26-27). Those who wish to get baptised must also be prepared to join themselves to a local church.

4.2 Subject Of Baptism

1 Baptism is to be administered to all who give a credible profession of faith. All the teaching on, and examples of, baptism in the New Testament involve those who have professed faith in Christ (Matt. 28:19-20; Mark 16:16; Acts 2:38, 41; 8:12; etc.). We require a *credible,* i.e. believable, profession of faith. We may be wrong in our judgment, but that does not mean that we should be lax in determining the faith of others. In the New Testament, baptism often followed immediately after profession of faith. At that time,

---

the pen?" When a student graduates from university, he wears a gown. We may ask, "What is the meaning of the gown?" The answer would be, "It indicates that the person wearing it has attained a certain standard in academic studies to qualify for a degree." We may also ask, "What is the purpose of wearing the gown?" The answer would be, "So that he may officially pass out of this university as one who is qualified in his field of studies."

While churches have disagreed about the meaning of baptism, they have agreed about the purpose of baptism. In practice, however, some churches baptise without requiring church membership. This is irregular, and should be done only in exceptional situations.

it was not fashionable to be a follower of Christ. In fact, it was potentially dangerous to be a Christian. Moreover, the apostles were around, and they had the extraordinary gift of discernment – to determine who were genuine believers and who were the hypocrites (Acts 5:1-11;8:9-25). Today, we would baptise as soon as it is convenient for the church, once we are sure of the person's conversion.

2 Infants of professing believers are not to be baptised because there is no command, no example, and no certain inference in the Holy Scriptures, to baptise them. To do so would be to:

(i) *Break the Regulative Principle.* In worship and church government, nothing must be introduced which is not taught in God's word (Dt. 12:32; Prov. 30:6; Lev. 10:1-2; 1689 Confession 1:6).

(ii) *Distort the Covenant of Grace.* God saves sinners by grace, through faith, in Christ (Eph. 2:8-9). It is not right to assume that infants born to believing parents are "covenant children". The Covenant of Grace cannot possibly encompass the non-elect, many of whom are found among the children of believing parents.

(iii) *Act contrary to the meaning and purpose of baptism.*

3 What of "Covenant Theology"? There is a true Covenant Theology which must not be confused with Paedobaptist Theology. The covenant made with Abraham must be understood not only by the light of the New Testament, but also by its development through the Old Testament. As revelation progressed, it became clearer and clearer that the Old Testament types and shadows were actually pointing to future spiritual realities involving the conversion of the Gentiles to faith in Christ, e.g. Jeremiah 31:31-34; Amos

9:11-12; Isaiah 60-66; etc. Note the following about Genesis 17:7-14:

(i) The true and spiritual seed of Abraham are those who have faith in Christ (Rom. 9:7; Gal. 3:7-9, 26-29).

(ii) The promised land pointed to the kingdom of God, or heaven (Gal. 5:21; Heb. 4:8-9; 11:8-16; 1 Pet. 1:4-5).

(iii) Circumcision pointed to regeneration, not baptism (Rom. 2:28-29; Col. 2:11-12). Baptism is a *new* sign of the *new* covenant (Heb. 8:7-13).

4 What about passages that seem to teach infant salvation?

(i) The "household passages": We are told in Acts 16: 31-34 that the Philippian jailer "rejoiced, having believed in God with all his household (v. 34)". Comparing 1 Corinthians 1:16 with 1 Corinthians 16:15, we discover that the household of Stephanas were the "firstfruits of Achaia", i.e. the first believers in Achaia. We are told also that "they have devoted themselves to the ministry of the saints", showing that all of them were believers. These instances should help us to understand the case of Lydia and her household (Acts 16:14-15). A fundamental rule of biblical interpretation is to proceed from what is clear to what is not clear.

(ii) Much has been made of the phrase, "For the promise is to you and to your children," in Acts 2:39. A fundamental rule of biblical interpretation is to understand the words in context. If Peter's immediate hearers needed to repent and be baptised in order to receive the gift of the Holy Spirit, why should their children receive the Spirit (or the covenant promise to Abraham) by some other way? Moreover, the last phrase in verse 39, "as many as the

Lord our God will call" qualifies all that preceded it. Whether Jews or Gentiles, all need to repent and have faith in Christ to be saved.

(iii) 1 Corinthians 7:14 has also been appealed to. There, the children of a believing parent is regarded as "holy" not in the sense that they are saved, but rather that they are "set apart" to be under the influence of the gospel, in contrast to those who are born in pagan families. Otherwise, the unbelieving partner , who is "sanctified" or "made holy" by the believing partner, would have to be regarded as saved as well. This would be contradictory to the way of salvation revealed in the Scripture. A word can take on more than one meaning in Scripture, e.g. "saved" in 1 Timothy 2:15, 1 Peter 3:21 and Mark 16:16. So also with the word "holy".

Those who use such passages to justify infant baptism are clutching at straw. Why not just submit to the clear teaching of Scripture?

4.3   The Mode Of Baptism

1 The correct way of baptising is by the immersion of the whole body in water, in the name of the Holy Trinity. This is based on the facts that:

(i) the word *baptizo* in Greek actually means "to dip, to submerge, or to immerse", not to sprinkle (*rhantizo*);

(ii) all the instances of actual baptism in the Bible support immersion, not sprinkling, of believers (Matt 3:16; Mark 1:9, 10; John 3:23; Acts 8:38, 39). Even the figurative baptisms carry the idea of being completely overwhelmed, thus supporting immersion (Mark 10:38-39; 1 Cor. 10:1-2; etc.). If we believe in the verbal inspiration of the Bible, we would have to accept the significance of going "down into the water" and coming "up out of the water", in such passages as Acts 8:38-39.

(iii) immersion alone correctly pictures our union with Christ in his burial and resurrection, and the washing away of our sins (e.g. Rom. 6:3-4; Col. 2:12; Acts 22:16).

2 In the past, paedobaptists argued pragmatically (some still do!) against immersion as the only mode, claiming that:

(i) The three thousand converted on the day of Pentecost could not have been immersed as that would have taken too much time. That is not a valid argument for, in practice, an immersion takes only a few seconds to perform. Moreover, we are not told that it was Peter alone who baptised. In all probability, all the apostles did the baptising, perhaps with the help of others (cf. John 4:1-2).

(ii) There wasn't any place good enough to immerse. But it is now known that there were so many large pools in the temple area, and many Roman baths scattered throughout Jerusalem. To be noted also is the fact that archaeology has uncovered many early baptisteries which were large, indicating immersion as the mode practised by the early church.[2]

3 What about those passages that seem to indicate that baptism is by some other mode?

(i) It has been argued that the ceremonial cleansing of the Jews in Mark 7:3-4 is described as baptisms, when no immersion was involved. We have already noted that the Greek word used here is *baptismos* (ceremonial cleansings) and not *baptisma* (the ordinance). Even in these ceremonial cleansings, total immersion was the mode, and not pouring.[2]

---

[2]Adamthwaite, RT 1989; Hulse, 1982.

(ii) It has also been argued that baptism may include other modes such as pouring since Spirit baptism, of which water baptism signifies, is described as "pouring" (Acts 2:17, 33, 38 cf. 1 Cor. 12:13). This, however, is an invalid argument. The words "pouring" and "baptism" in these passages are used figuratively, and they are two different words. The meaning of a word must not be determined from its figurative usage, much less from a parallel word that is also used figuratively. For example, in John 11:11-13, the word "sleep" is used figuratively to refer to death. We do not conclude from this that "sleep" literally means death!

4 As to the element in which baptism is to be performed, water is water – whether still, running, muddy or salty. The main thing is that the meaning and purpose of baptism are not violated.

4.4   The Importance of Baptism

1 Baptism is not essential to salvation. It is nevertheless important to the Christian and the church because of the following considerations:

(i) Baptism is clearly a matter of duty since it is taught in such passages as Matthew 28:18-20 and Acts 2:38. We are therefore obliged to determine the biblical practice, and follow it. There is, after all, "one Lord, one faith, *one baptism*" (Eph. 4:5).

(ii) Discipleship, and the lordship of Christ over us, demand that we take baptism seriously. As we grow in the grace and knowledge of our Lord Jesus Christ, we must grow in obedience to His teachings, right down to matters that are regarded as unimportant by others (cf. 1 Sam. 15:22).

(iii) The doctrine of the local church demands that we take baptism seriously. The local church is central and unique in the purposes of God. Each local church is held directly accountable to the Lord for its purity – in doctrine and practice (Rev. 1-3). The visible church is to consist of baptised believers who voluntarily covenant together to observe the ordinances of the gospel.

2 In the face of the clear teaching of Scripture on baptism, it will not do for believers to be "neither here nor there". We have to ask, How many modes of baptism are there? How many subjects of baptism are there? How many ways of salvation are there? A person who has been sprinkled before is not getting "rebaptised" when he undergoes immersion, but is being baptised for the first time.

Questions

1 Was the Ethiopian eunuch baptised into membership of a local church (Acts 8)? What lessons may we draw out of this incident?

2 What difficulties are there to baptising a person immediately upon profession of faith? When is it right to do so?

3 How would you answer those who say that the only condition of church membership is faith in Christ, and therefore the mode of baptism is unimportant?

References

1 Adamthwaite, Murray. 1989. Reformation Today, Issue No. 109.

2 Hulse, Erroll. 1982. The Testimony of Baptism. Carey Pubs.

Five

THE LORD'S SUPPER
(1 Cor. 10:14-22; 11:17-34)

The Lord's Supper is a special (or holy) ordinance of the local church. Just as church discipline instituted in the presence of the apostles was meant for New Testament churches (Matt. 18:15-17), so also the Lord's Supper (1 Cor. 11:18, 23ff.). It should therefore be conducted in the context of a local church gathering, and under the proper discipline and supervision of the local church.

5.1 Meaning And Purpose

As with baptism, the Lord's Supper has its meaning and purpose.

1 *Meaning:* Symbolically to show forth –

(i) Christ's death (1 Cor. 11:23-26);

(ii) Our participation in His death, and therefore, also in His resurrection (1 Cor. 10:16; Rom. 6:5).

2 *Purpose:* It is multi-pronged –

(i) To remember the Lords death (Luke 22:19; 1 Cor. 11:24, 25).

(ii) As a public and symbolic proclamation of the gospel (1 Cor. 11:26).

(iii) To strengthen our faith, love, obedience, and commitment (1 Cor. 10:21; 5:7-8).

(iv) To engage in self-examination, repentance, and resolve to live a holier life (1 Cor. 10:27, 28, 31).

(v) To express our fellowship with one another because of our union with Christ (1 Cor. 10:16-17).

3 From the meaning and purpose of the ordinance we may determine how frequently it should be celebrated.

(i) The passover feast, which foreshadowed the Lord's Supper, was celebrated only once in a year. From this, it would seem that we are not to have the Lord's Supper so regularly that its special significance is lost. The words, "This do, as often as you drink it (1 Cor. 11:25)," also indicate that it is not intended to be celebrated too often.

(ii) On the other hand, we are told to do it in remembrance of the Lord. Surely, we would like to remember the Lord often. Furthermore, this is a means of grace. It is to be done for the good of our soul.

We conclude that it must be done frequently enough, but not so frequently as to lose its special significance. To have it once a week is to have it too frequently. To have it once in three months would be too infrequent since a church member who is providentially hindered from partaking in one would have to wait another three months for the next one. In our church, we have it once a fortnight.

5.2   The Participants

1 Who may participate in the Lord's Supper? Should it be opened
   to all who are present in the church meeting, or should it be restricted to church members? We believe that it should be opened
   to:

   (i) Baptised believers. This is because it is a church ordinance, and
   therefore meant for members. Moreover, the biblical order is to
   be observed: baptism into membership, followed by communion
   (Matt. 28:19-20; Acts 2:41-42).

   (ii) Visiting believers who are in good standing with their churches.
   This is because one purpose of the Lord's Supper is to express
   fellowship, and surely we should express fellowship with visiting
   brethren who are walking in obedience to the Lord.

   This is "restricted communion", in contrast to "open communion"
   in which all who are present may partake, and "strict/closed communion" in which only baptised believers of the church, or of like-
   minded churches, are allowed to partake.

2 The church should announce clearly who may partake in the ordinance before it is celebrated. Visitors who have introduced themselves in advance and are known to be in good standing with their
   home-churches should be invited personally by the elders. Those
   known to be under church discipline should be excluded.

3 Convinced paedobaptists and other believers who are not members, although attending the church regularly, should consult the
   elders so that some arrangements may be made for them to take
   the Lord's Supper. Different churches hold to different views about
   the participation of such believers. The difficulties revolve around
   the two factors of: (a) the need to maintain the Lord's Supper as

a church ordinance; and (b) the need to express fellowship with all true believers. Over the years, we have decided to be generous and allow such to partake.

4 Conditions are attached to participation in the Lord's Supper:

(i) Self-examination, to ensure that one is a true believer (1 Cor. 11:28-29; 2 Cor. 13:5).

(ii) To take worthily, i.e. knowing its meaning and purpose. Note: With the conditions is a warning of God's judgment (1 Cor. 11:28-29, 30-32).

5.3   The Mode

How should the Lord's Supper be conducted? Different churches do it differently, but three considerations should be borne in mind.

1 *The elements:* We must follow the "simplicity" given in 1 Corinthians 11 and not strive for detail. In verse 23, bread is bread everywhere: whether made from rye, wheat, white, wholemeal, leavened or unleavened, flat or round. In verse 25, the cup: nothing is specified. From the Gospels, we know that it was "fruit of the vine". This could be very inclusive: any fruit juice. After all, it is but a symbol; the importance rests in what is symbolised.

It is sometimes argued that the Lord's Supper is a replacement of the Jewish passover feast, just as baptism is a replacement of circumcision. It follows that only unleavened bread should be used in the Lord's Supper since leaven represents sin. The New Testament, however, shows that the taking away of leaven pointed to the taking away of our sins by the Lord Jesus Christ (1 Cor. 5:7-8), just as circumcision of the flesh pointed to the circumcision of the heart, i.e. regeneration (Col. 2:11-12). In other words, both ordinances are meant to symbolically proclaim the gospel or, in the words of Keach's Catechism, "to represent and apply to believers the benefits of the new covenant". Just as circumcision of the flesh should not be directly equated with baptism, the passover feast should not be directly equated with the Lord's Supper. Baptism and the Lord's Supper are new ordinances of the new covenant (Heb. 8). These relations may be shown by diagram as in Fig.5.1.

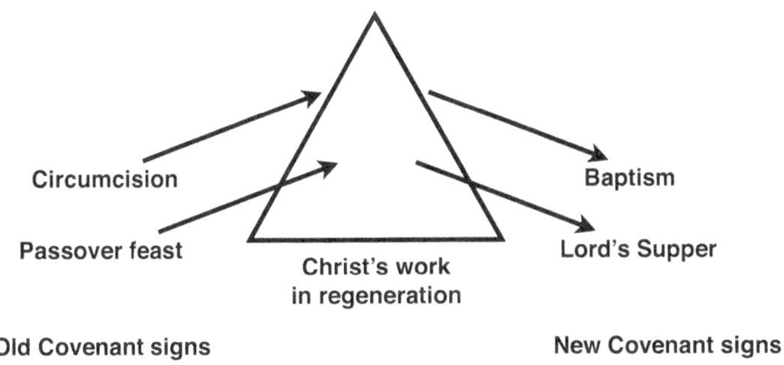

Fig. 5.1: Old Covenants Signs And New Covenant Signs

2 *The symbol:* Ideally, the single cup and single loaf is to be preferred, but circumstances might make this impractical, e.g. when the congregation is large. The "one loaf' is a symbol of unity (1 Cor. 10:17), which surely is achieved when those of a common interest engage simultaneously in eating and drinking the elements with a common purpose. However, in most situations, the one cup and one loaf should be possible. Note that the one cup is to be "divided" or "distributed" (Luke 22:17, 20). In other words, the in-

dividual cups are filled from a bigger cup, or jug. In practice, little communion cups may be filled in advance except for one, which is filled before all of them are distributed, to show that the content of all has come from the one big cup.

3 *The administration:* It is the minister's responsibility to give thanks for the elements before they are distributed. (See 28:2; 30:3 of the 1689 Confession.) Others may be *delegated* to pray for the elements, but the *responsibility* to do that rests with the minister. That being the case, it would be best that the minister does it most of the time. In the original institution of the ordinance, the Lord Himself blessed the elements. Furthermore, the ordinance is meant to be a public and symbolic proclamation of the gospel, which duty belongs mainly to the minister.

5.4   Its Importance To The Church And The Believer

1 As with baptism, we would practise what we believe are clearly taught in the Bible. What we are not clear about, we would not insist, e.g. the type of water, whether running, fresh, or salty; the type of bread, whether leavened or unleavened. Overemphasis on non-essentials can lead to the errors of the Pharisees: traditionalism and quibbling over unnecessary details (Matt. 23:23; Mark 7:8).

2 Differences concerning the mode should not break fellowship between churches. Differences concerning the subject and the meaning and purpose are more serious. That is why we cannot have fellowship with the Roman Catholic Church, which perverts the ordinance into an enactment of the sacrifice of Christ, the ele-

ments of which are "transubstantiated" (changed into actual flesh and blood), and the partaking of which is supposed to impart salvation. Our convictions lead to our practices. We expect others to respect us as a church, just as we do other true churches.

3 Do not take this special ordinance lightly. And, do not take church membership lightly. It is impossible to be a "visitor" for ever! If there are any doubts about doctrine or practice, get them cleared soon. Join the church as a member. Enjoy the privilege of sitting at the Lord's table together with other brothers and sisters in Christ, in full and perfect fellowship!

Questions

1 Some believers are not members of the church due to circumstances, and not by choice. Should the Lord's Supper be opened to them?

2 Should the Lord's Supper be conducted during our Annual Combined Church Camp, in which a number of churches are represented?

3 As with baptism, the Lord's Supper has been "a bone of contention" in church history. Discuss the danger of: (i) making it an "idol"; (ii) treating it as unimportant.

Six

PRAYER (Matt. 6:5-15)

Prayer can be individual or corporate. When an individual believer prays, he is worshipping God, and expressing dependence and trust in Him. This is what it means to "call on the name of the Lord" (cf. Rom. 10:13; Gen. 12:8; 13:4; 21:33). Prayer shows whether a person is a Christian or not, and whether he is spiritually healthy. It may be compared with breathing. A person breathes because he is alive. He breathes well and regularly when he is healthy.

Our concern here is with corporate prayer. Just as individual prayer indicates the health of the believer, corporate prayer is a good indication of the health of a local church. Apart from other things, the early church was characterised by corporate prayer (Acts 2:42; 4:23-31).

6.1   On Corporate Prayer

We shall consider the attitude involved in corporate prayer, the content of our prayers, and the manner by which corporate prayer should be conducted.

1 *The Attitude:*

(i) As with other aspects of the Christian or church life, prayer is a God-centred activity. This needs to be emphasised because man-centred thinking prevails. Many take prayer as a psychological crutch, done to "make you feel better". It also leads to abuse, e.g. using it as a platform to "tell somebody something". If kept God-centred, the following will be true:

    (a) We will pray believingly;

    (b) We will trust God to hear us;

    (c) We will pray with the end of glorifying God.

(ii) Many people are troubled by the apparent contradiction between God's sovereignty and human responsibility. This is what has been called an "antinomy" – an apparent incompatibility between two truths. God has commanded us to pray, yet He acts according to His sovereign will.[1] The Lord has promised that if we ask anything in His name, He will do it (John 14:13-14; 16:23-24). We must believe that promise and pray. Our prayers will be answered in ways that do not contradict the sovereignty of God. C. H. Spurgeon was once asked if he could reconcile divine sovereignty with human responsibility, to which he gave the reply: "I wouldn't try. I never reconcile friends."

2 *The Content:* The Lord's Prayer (Matt. 6:9-13; Luke 11:2-4) serves as our model, and no more (Luke 11:1, 2). We are not to recite it as liturgy, although that is not wrong in some special situations.

---

[1]My preference is to see human responsibility as subsumed under divine sovereignty. In other words, God's sovereignty includes and involves human responsibility. Therefore, there is no tension between divine sovereignty and human responsibility, while divine sovereignty is allowed to be what it is – the almighty God in control over all.

"The Shorter Catechism" and "Keach's Catechism" give the meaning of each petition in the Lord's Prayer. Here, we make some of of own observations:

(i) As a general rule, prayer is directed to God the Father (Matt. 6:9), in the name of the Son (John 14:13, 14), by the power of the Spirit (Rom. 8:26, 27). See also John 16:23, 26-27. It is not wrong under certain circumstances, to pray to the Son or the Spirit. To pray "in Christ's name" means to pray in accordance to the revealed will of God which centres around Christ. It means also to pray by Christ's authority, based on His finished work on the cross.

(ii) There is praise and adoration of God, because of who He is (Matt. 6:9).

(iii) There is prayer for God's rule to extend on earth, for His cause to be advanced, for His purposes to be fulfilled (v. 10).

(iv) We pray for legitimate needs in this life (v. 11).

(v) We pray for the forgiveness of sins and for a clear conscience based on the merits of Christ (v. 12).

(vi) We pray for help to live a pure, godly, and righteous life (v. 13).

(vii) We express our dependence and trust in God, and desiring His glory (v. 13).

3 *The Manner:*

(i) Corporate prayer is uttered prayer (Acts 1:24-25; 4:24ff. 1 Kings 8:22ff.). It is not silent meditation, as the Roman Catholics believe. It is not liturgy, i.e. reciting printed prayers, as the Anglicans believe. It is not everyone praying his own prayer aloud at the same time, the method popularised by John Sung.[2] In Acts

4:24, "...they raised their voice to God with one accord and said...", simply means they were united in heart, with someone leading in prayer, and not everyone uttering a prayer in unison. We know this because:

> (a) The phrase "with one accord" is used elsewhere to mean "united in heart" (e.g. Acts 2:46);

> (b) Only one prayer is recorded, not many that were uttered in unison;

> (c) There is no example in the Bible of corporate prayer in the "John Sung style", but there are numerous examples of someone praying on behalf of the others present;

> (d) There is clear teaching that anything uttered by more than one person must be done each in turn (1 Cor. 14:15-17, 27-32).

(ii) Not every item needs to be mentioned by every individual. Keep it brief and to the point. Remember, others need to pray as well!

(iii) Vain repetitions – of words, phrases, items – are to be avoided (Matt. 6:7).

(iv) Prayer should be led, and done in turn. Led, because when one prays, he is praying on behalf of others (cf. Acts 1:24-25; 4:24ff; 20:36). The "Amen" should be loud and clear (1 Cor. 14:16). In turn, because of the principles of understanding and edification (1 Cor. 14:12-17), and the principle of decency and order (1 Cor. 14:40 cf. 27). This is not observed today in many Charismatic or pro-Charismatic churches.

---

[2] Tow, 1985:114).

(iv) Various postures are possible: bowing down the head (Gen. 24:26, 27); prostration on the ground (Gen. 17:17); kneeling (Acts 20:36; 21:5); hands raised (1 Kings 8:22, 54; Luke 24:50). In Nehemiah 8:6, three different postures are adopted. The important thing is an attitude of humility, reverence and awe, which surely is shown when heads are bowed and eyes are closed. Eyes closed also helps in our concentration, although this is not always possible, e.g. when one is praying through a list of names and items; when one prays while having a walk.

(v) Fervency or earnestness is not something that is "put on", but flows from a heart that believes and has feelings.

6.2   Other Relevant Comments

1 In corporate prayer, participation is most needed but least attempted. It is better to have "clashes" of more than one person wanting to pray than to have few praying, or long lapses of silence between prayers. The principle of privacy (Matt. 6:6) applies to individual and corporate prayers. In other words, those who pray should not parade themselves to the public. When in a prayer meeting, that principle should not be made an excuse for not praying (Acts 1:14; 2:42:4:23, 31).

2 The error of Sandemanianism ("only by faith" is taken to mean intellectual assent, without conviction of heart, or feelings)[3] is shown most clearly in prayer by the lack of fervency or earnestness. Contrast this with the prayers of Elijah, Nehemiah, Daniel, and the Lord in 1 Kings 17:20, 21; 18:36, 37; Nehemiah 1:4-11; Daniel 9:4-19; and Luke 22:41-44.

---

[3]This view was propagated by Robert Sandeman (1718-1771) in Britain.

3 There are various ways of dealing with big groups, e.g. splitting up into smaller groups first before coming together again; or calling upon a number of people to pray for requested items at intervals. The problem is often poor attendance rather than having too many persons present.

4 Prayer is an act of worship. It may be stimulated by a short Bible reading before the meeting. It may be enhanced by reading a Psalm and short hymns, interspersed between the prayers. It is fuelled by information. Items for prayer may be read out, a few slides of missionary situations, and people to be prayed for, may be shown before the meeting.

5 Some churches do not permit ladies to pray. We are of a different opinion, believing that the prayer meeting is a family gathering in which the ladies must be encouraged to pray. Acts 1:14 would seem to emphasise, instead of prohibit, the participation of women. Of course, the general principle of male leadership should be observed: a man should chair the meeting, and one or two men present should pray before the women do so.

Questions

1 What are some of the reasons for poor attendance at the church prayer meeting? Are they legitimate? How may they be overcome?

2 How may our church prayer meetings be improved? Is there a link between corporate prayer and private prayer?

3 Discuss the relative importance of missions and outreach items, compared to other matters such as personal needs, at the prayer meeting.

Reference

1 Tow, Timothy. 1985. John Sung My Teacher. Christian Life Publishers.

Seven

Worship (1 Cor. 14:20-40)

The word "worship" comes from "worth-ship". It means to express "worth-ship", or reverence, to God, to pay homage to Him. Worship is both an individual as well as a corporate matter:

i The individual believer should lead a life of worship (1 Cor. 6:19-20). He should also engage in acts of worship, namely prayer, reading the Scripture, and singing praises to God. Those who are married should also have family worship at home. The Shorter Catechism says, "The chief end of man is to glorify God and to enjoy Him forever." This is what fallen man fails to do (Rom. 1:20-21).

ii The church should, as a body, worship God. Romans 12: says, "I beseech you therefore, brethren, by the mercies of God that you present your bodies a living sacrifice, holy, acceptable to God, which is your reasonable service." The word for "service" (Greek, *latreia*) actually means worship. Note that the word "sacrifice" is in the singular. This shows that all the members of the church should give themselves as a body to serve, or worship, God.

God sanctioned worship in the local church (Acts 2:42-41 20:7; Heb. 10:25). This is to prepare us for worship in heaven (Rev. 4:8-11; 5:9-14; 7:9-12).

7.1 Principles That Should Govern Worship

1 *The Regulative Principle:* This states that the worship of God should be conducted according to whatever is taught in the Bible whether by commands, precepts, examples, or principles. The Regulative Principle is upheld by churches of the Reformed and Evangelical tradition. The opposing principle, sometimes called (inappropriately) the Normative Principle,[1] states that whatever is not forbidden by Scripture is allowable. This is followed by Anglicans, Lutherans, Roman Catholics, and modern Evangelicals.

(i) The Regulative Principle is taught in the Old Testament (e.g. Dt. 12:32; Lev. 10:1-3), and continues to be applicable to us although the way of worship has been abolished in Christ (Heb. 8-10).

(ii) The Regulative Principle is also taught in the New Testament (Matt. 28:20; Mark 7:6-8; Col. 2:23; Rev. 22:18-19). No human tradition or innovation is to be introduced.

(iii) This principle takes into account things indifferent, which are connected with the circumstances of worship, e.g. the time and duration of worship, the order of worship, whether the congregation should be seated, standing or kneeling, etc. Such matters should be decided by sanctified common sense, and the general

---

[1] The "Normative Principle" should be another name for the Regulative Principle since the Scripture sets the "norm" for us to follow. The opposing principle should be called the Permissive Principle since it states that whatever is not forbidden in Scripture is allowable or permissible.

principles taught in Scripture – e.g. to do all things to the glory of God, for the edification of the church, decently and in order, without stumbling weaker brethren and non-believers (1 Cor. 10:23, 31; 14:40; Rom. 14:13).

2 *In spirit and truth (John 4:24):*

(i) *In spirit* means in a spiritual manner, and in sincerity of heart (cf. Matt. 15:8-9).

(ii) *In truth* means in accordance to the teaching of Scripture, based on the finished work of Christ (2 Tim. 3:16-17; Heb. 10:19-22). It also means that the mind should be actively involved (cf. 1 Cor. 14:15-17).

3 *God-centred instead of man-centred (Matt. 4:10):* A God-centred approach will prevent the worship from degenerating into mere entertainment. It will also prevent the worshippers from thinking only of what they may gain out of the service.

4 *To be conducted decently and in order (1 Cor. 14:40):* Normally, the hymns must be chosen and arranged in advance, and the message prepared well. We are not discounting the need to be flexible as circumstances demand, nor the possibility of the Holy Spirit prompting the preacher to utter words unplanned for. We are only saying that the general rule of decency and order should be observed.

5 *In simplicity:* Instead of showiness and external pomp, things should be done spiritually and from the heart (2 Cor. 1:12; 11:3; cf. Rev. 4-5). This last reference concerns worship in heaven which will be touched on again below.

7.2   How Worship Is To Be Conducted

1 *The attitude:*

(i) Reverently, because we are approaching a holy and majestic God.

(ii) Humbly, because we are sinners and creatures.

(iii) Joyfully, because we are a redeemed people.

(iv) Spiritually, because it is a spiritual activity, not a worldly or carnal one.

(v) Prayerfully, because we are dependent upon God for everything.

2 *The elements:*

(i) Bible reading; preaching; prayers; singing of psalms, hymns and spiritual songs; the Lord's Supper; collection (Acts 2:42; 1 Tim. 4:13; Eph. 5:19; 1 Cor. 11:23-34; 16:2). Of these, prayer and preaching appear to be the irreducible minimum of public worship (1 Tim. 1-4; 1 Cor. 14, esp. vs. 24-25). Prayer is men calling upon God, while preaching is God speaking to men.

(ii) Note that there are no more prophesies and tongues, but the principles in 1 Corinthians 14:26-40 still apply, namely, edification, the use of the mind, decency and order, and the respective roles of men and women.

3 *The manner:*

(i) Worship should be led. This was the case in the Old Testament (Lev. 1; 2 Chron. 6:12: Neh. 8), in the synagogues, in the early church, right through the history of the church, until recent years. The "free-for-all" situation in Corinth was censured by Paul (1 Cor. 14:26ff.), but is advocated by many today.

(ii) Whole-hearted participation by everyone present – singing hymns, hearing preaching, saying the "Amen" (cf. 1 Cor. 14:16). Hearing the word preached may be considered the highest act of worship, since the people quietly and reverently hear what God has to say to them.

(iii) The "hymn sandwich" format fits the requirement to do all things decently and in order, yet keeps the worshippers attentive and involved. It is only right that we should pattern our worship after that in heaven (Rev. 4-5). Note the singing of praises in Revelation 4:8, 11; 5:9, 12, and 13, between which are the other items of worship.

(iv) We use the word "hymns" to cover the "psalms, hymns and spiritual songs" referred to in Ephesians 5:19 and Colossians 3:16.[2] The content should be God-centred, biblical, evangelical (i.e. consistent with the gospel of "Christ and Him crucified") and rich in theological content. The tunes used should be in accord with the attitude of worship spelled out above.

(v) The primacy of the word of God requires that preaching should be the climax of the worship service. The hymns should be chosen such that they prepare the hearers for the message, and are the response of the hearers to the message. The Lord's Supper, important though it is, should not be the prime focus of the ser-

---

[2]Some churches sing only the Psalms, believing that the Regulative Principle requires this, since the "psalms, hymns and spiritual songs" of Ephesians 5:19 and Colossians 3:16 are different words used in reference to the Psalms. We reject this narrow application of the Regulative Principle because: (i) we believe that the words refer to various types of songs sung in praise to God; (ii) the book of Psalms is primarily Scripture, and not a song book, to New Testament believers; (iii) although there is a continuity between the Old Testament and the New Testament, the discontinuity should also be noted (Matt. 9:16-17; Acts 2:17, 21; Heb. 8:7ff.), which requires that we sing new songs related to the new covenant (cf. Rev. 5:9); (iv) unlike reading of Scripture and preaching, singing and praying are the responses of men to the truths of God's word heard.

vice. Singing should not predominate over preaching. The music should not predominate over the words sung.[3]

(iv) As far as possible, worship should be conducted on a Sunday, since this is the Christian sabbath or the Lord's day (Exod. 20:8-11 cf. Acts 2:1; 20:7; 1 Cor. 16:2). Keeping the sabbath is itself an act of worship. Whenever possible, worship may be conducted on other days as well (cf. Acts 2:42; 5:42).

7.3 Preparation For Worship

1 Sleep early on Saturday night to be fresh the following day. Clear all work and prepare for the following day: petrol for car, ingredients for Sunday meals, washing and ironing, sweeping the floor, baby things collected together, etc.

2 Be on time for worship. Hurry causes mindlessness – an unprepared state to worship.

3 Correctness in form without the powerful presence of God's Spirit is useless. No doubt, God is present wherever His people are gathered in His name (Matt. 18:20), but it is another thing to have His special presence.

Questions

1 What biblical warrant is there for the use of musical instruments in worship today? What principles should govern their use? Many

---

[3]We believe that musical instruments of the appropriate types may be used in aid of worship, although worship need not be the worse for want of music. This is for the reasons that: (i) in the Bible, singing almost always presumes the use of musical instruments; (ii) certain musical instruments were used in the worship of the Old Testament; (iii) the word "psalms" denote songs that have musical accompaniment.

churches are already using pop-bands in worship. What can you say about that?

2 How are we to view the repetitious choruses sung in many churches today? Need we use only old hymns and old tunes?

3 Can you suggest practical ways of maintaining or improving the standard of worship in our own church?

Eight

Evangelism (Acts 2:40-47)

Acts 2:47 reads, "...praising God and having favour with all the people. And the Lord added to the church daily those who were being saved." This indicates clearly that evangelism was part-and-parcel of life in the early church. The full implications of the Great Commission might not have been grasped yet, but the church obviously remembered it (cf. v. 40). The early believers lived in close interaction with other people. They were obviously proclaiming the gospel frequently and spontaneously, so that many of the hearers were being saved daily. Winning souls to Christ was so much a part of their lives that when persecution arose later, "those who were scattered went everywhere preaching the word (Acts 8:4)."

8.1   The Necessity For Evangelism

1 The Great Commission is binding upon all Christians in all generations (Matt. 28:18-20).

(i) Note "all nations", "with you always, to the end of the age". These could not have applied to the apostles alone.

(ii) Other passages in the New Testament also show its abiding relevance (Matt. 5:14-16; Phil. 2:15; Rom. 10:8-17 cf. Acts 2:21).

(iii) The importance and urgency of the task is shown by the repetition of the command (Mark 16:15; Luke 24:46-47; Acts 1:8), which was given in the period before the Lord was taken to heaven.

(iv) This is a command given to disciples gathered together *as a church*. As long as there are churches in this world, there is a responsibility to proclaim the gospel.

2　The Great Commission is a command to the local church, to plant local churches. Note:

(i) The gathered apostles were the church "in embryo". The church was born on the day of Pentecost (cf. Matt. 18:17). The apostles were also representatives of the New Testament churches, so that a command given to them was also a command to the local churches. This becomes clear when we compare with the institution of the Lord's Supper (Luke 22:14-22 cf. 1 Cor. 11:23 ff.).

(ii) The Great Commission consists of the imperative (i.e. the command) "*make disciples of* all the nations", and three participles which show how it is to be done: "*going* (into the world)", "*baptising* them in the name of the Holy Trinity", and "*teaching* them to keep all the Lord's commandments".

(iii) The examples of the early churches show that this is the correct understanding of the Great Commission. Paul founded churches in his missionary journeys. Peter and others were doing the same (1 Cor. 9:5; Acts 9:31-32ff.).

8.2   Evangelism Conducted By The Church

1 Evangelism should be conducted in three main ways:

(i) *Organised:* The Lord did this (Mark 6:6, 7ff.; Luke 10:1ff). Specially-gifted people should be sent farther afield (Acts 13:1-3; Rom. 10:15; 16:6ff.; 1 Cor. 9:5). Note the roles of women in gospel work, under the leadership of men, and when accompanying their husbands.

(ii) *Spontaneous:* Carried out by every member (Acts 2:47; 5:13-14; 8:4; etc.). This often prepared the ground for the ministers to sow and reap (Acts 8:4-5).

(iii) *In the regular ministry of the church:* See 2 Tim. 4:5; 1 Cor. 14:24-25. It is important that the main meetings of the church have an evangelistic thrust. Members must go out to preach. They must also invite people to church to hear the pastor preach.

2 Evangelism is effective when those engaged in it are clear of:

(i) The relation between God's sovereignty and human responsibility. We must not be crippled by Hyper-Calvinism or Arminianism.

(ii) The doctrines of grace. Our message should be full-orbed, balanced, proportioned to the understanding of the hearers, and true.

(iii) The order of salvation. This will help us to discern true conviction of sin, repentance, and faith, and how best to minister to the hearers.

3 The nature of evangelism should be clearly understood:

(i) *The attitude:* Desire to glorify God by obedience to Him should be the primary motive (Matt. 28:18-20; 1 Cor. 10:31). Love for men should flow from a love of God (Matt. 22:37-39; 9:36; 2 Cor. 5:14).

(ii) *The content:* Focus upon Christ and the cross (1 Cor. 1:23; 2:2; Acts 4:12).

(iii) *The means:* The proclamation of the gospel (Rom. 10:14, 17), and prayer for the hearers to be saved (1 Cor. 3:7) go hand-in-hand. Paul taught, preached, disputed, reasoned, persuaded, and prayed. There must be people to hear the proclaimed message, whether in a group or individually. Souls must be sought out. Effort must be made to go to people. Earnestness, consistency of life, true love for sinners -these will go a long way to help win souls.

(iv) *The method:* Outreach teams should be formed consisting of two to five persons (Mark 6:7; Luke 10:1; Acts 20:4-5), led by a man, to visit groups/households on a regular basis (Acts 20:20; Matt. 10:11-14) – until souls are converted or the preachers are unwanted. Often, a ten-minutes gospel message from an open Bible is sufficient, followed by a brief prayer. When a hunger for God's word develops, two or more groups/households may be joined together to become a preaching point (Acts 17:2-9; 18:4-8; 19:8-10; 20:20-21). The seekers and the converts are introduced to the church, coming to worship together, say, once a month, until they are baptised and integrated with the membership. When the preaching point is far from the church, the converts are baptised and prepared for covenanting together as a new church.

4 Concern for growth of the local church should lead to concern for church planting. One is the extension of the other, and belong together in the Great Commission. Local church growth and wider church planting are complementary activities, each helping the

other (2 Cor. 10:13-16). Church leaders should take the lead in church planting, and church members should be supportive of them in this.

8.3   Some Concluding Points

1 Wrong beliefs and approaches to evangelism abound today. Such evangelism tends to be Arminian, activist, ecumenical, and based in para-church organisations.[1] We must be careful not to over-react to these errors by:

(i) Failing to be involved in "aggressive evangelism", i.e. actively bringing the gospel to others. If there is no sowing of the seed of the gospel, there will be no harvest of souls.

(ii) Concentrating on building up the faith of believers without a strong emphasis on soul-winning. Both are important. In Matthew 28:19-20, the new disciples are baptised into membership of the church, and then built up in the faith. In 1 Timothy 3:15, the church is both the pillar as well as the ground (or foundation) of the truth – the pillar to hold up high the gospel in this spiritually

---

[1] Arminians hold to the view that Christ died for every individual in the world, instead of just for the elect. They therefore believe that it is now up to the individual to "decide for Christ" in order to be saved. Often, this means doing something – such as walking to the front of the church or raising the hand – to indicate acceptance of Christ as Saviour. Hence, salvation becomes the work of Christ *plus* the work of the individual!

The man-centredness in today's evangelism is also seen in the activistic approach in which there is much noise and drama, but little preaching of the glorious truths of the gospel. As a consequence, there are many who profess faith, but few who are soundly converted.

Ecumenical-minded Christians have no qualms about working together with those who hold to questionable beliefs. All this is done in the name of "Christian unity".

Many para-church organisations exist to evangelise the lost but are not concerned about the centrality and uniqueness of the local church in the purposes of God.

dark world, and the foundation upon which the faith of converts are built up. Those whose faith are being built up will be keen to win souls.

(iii) Building up the local church without engaging in church-planting. Ideally, each local church should have a number of local outreach groups in the vicinity, and a satellite work farther afield. The church in Corinth had other satellite groups scattered throughout Achaia (1 Cor. 1:2; 2 Cor. 1:1). The church in Ephesus spawned a number of churches in its vicinity (Rev. 1:11, 20; Acts 4:13, 16). The church in Jerusalem sent out Peter, Philip, and other preachers to establish the faith of scattered believers and to plant churches (Acts 8:5; 10:32ff.; 1 Cor. 9:5). The church at Antioch sent out Paul and other missionaries to plant churches (Acts 13:2-3; 15:36, 40-41).

2 The fulfillment of the divine purpose must be grasped – the calling out of the elect from all nations by the preaching of the gospel (Isa. 60:1-3; 62:2, 10-12; Matt. 9:37-38; John 12:24, 32; Acts 2:17, 21; Eph. 1:3-14; Rev. 7:9-10). Let us be soul-winners!

Questions

1 Suggest some reasons why Christians shrink from the task of evangelism. How may these problems be overcome?

2 Home evangelistic meetings appear to be the method honoured by God in the time of the apostles (consider the "household" passages, Acts 10; 16:15 cf. 40; 16:31-34; 28:30-31). How relevant is this method today, and to our situation?

3 Every believer should be a potential candidate for missionary service. Give reasons why you should not be sent out as a missionary of the church!

Nine

Support Of The Ministry (1 Cor. 9:1-18)

We are here referring to the office and work of the pastor. Wrong views of the ministry prevail. Many people have the idea that:

i The pastor is a super-spiritual person. He has no problems of health, family, and personal needs. He has renounced the material world to live a frugal life. He is expected to put up with financial difficulties, work without holidays, and remain healthy always.

ii His livelihood is miraculously supported by God. The pastor is amply supplied by gifts from Christians, over and above his minimum pay.

iii His work is "only preaching and prayers" and he has plenty of free time. He should therefore be ready to do the mundane things in the church, e.g. cleaning the toilet. He is expected to be helpful to others, and may therefore be called upon to run errands.

9.1 A Right View Of The Ministry

1 A full-time ministry is not essential to the *being* of the church, but it is essential to its *well-being*. The first churches did not have full-time ministers (Acts 14:21-23 cf. 9:31). However, very early on, full-time ministry was established (Eph. 4:11-12; 2 Tim. 2:2; 1 Tim. 5:17ff.).

2 A minister's life and work are not enviable in many ways:

(i) He has the awesome responsibility of being a representative of Christ, fulfilling the duties as prophet, priest, and king (1 Pet. 5:1-4; Rev. 1:20; 2:1). He preaches to, prays for, and rules over, the household of God.

(ii) The two matters he primarily deals with are delicate and intense at the same time – the word of God (2 Tim. 2:15; James 3:1), and the people of God (Eph. 5:25-27; Acts 20:28-30; Luke 17:2).

(iii) He has to set an example in every area of his life – in his family (1 Tim. 3:4-5); in his personal life (1 Tim. 4:12); in ruling the church (1 Pet. 5:3); in his walk in society (1 Tim. 3:7).

(iv) Responsibilities in the church are not only heavy, but also many – prayer, preaching and teaching, spiritual oversight, evangelism, studies, guarding the church, rebuking errors, etc. (Acts 6:4; 20:29; 1 Tim. 4:13; 5:17; 2 Tim. 4:5; Tit. 3:10-11). A minister is a servant *to* the church. He is not a servant *of* the church. He is fulfilling a call, not engaging in a hobby.

3 The ministry must be supported by the church members through:

(i) constant prayer (1 Tim. 2:7-8; 2 Thess. 3:1; Col. 4:3; Heb 13:18);

(ii) submission (Heb. 13:7; 17; 2 Thess. 5:12-13);

(iii) finance (1 Tim. 5:17-18; 1 Cor. 9:9, 14; Gal. 6:6).

All these are important, but the last is the least talked about and the least understood.

9.2   Financial Support Of The Ministry

1 To what extent is the minister to be financially supported? It should be ample, so that:

(i) It constitutes "a living", or "livelihood" (1 Cor. 9:14), and "double honour" (1Tim. 5:17).

(ii) Every department of his life may be reasonably catered for, i.e. "in all good things" (Gal. 6:6) – family life, children's education, holidays, hospitality, travels, petrol, telephone bills, books and magazines, etc.

(iii) He is not to be unnecessarily entangled or distracted by worldly affairs (2 Tim. 2:4-6).

2 The church need not fear over-paying the pastor since, if truly called of God, he will not be serving for dishonest gain (1 Pet. 5:2; 1 Tim. 6:5). Any excess fund he receives will be channeled to the Lord's work. In a pioneering situation, the preacher might *voluntarily* abstain from having ample or any pay (Acts 18:3; 20:34-35; 1 Cor. 9:6; cf. Phil. 4:10-20).

3 The support of the ministry, as well as of other gospel works, will be no problem if church members are giving to the Lord correctly. Principles of Christian giving include the following:

(i) *Who should give?* All believers, whether rich or poor (Gal. 6:6; 2 Cor. 8:1-2; Luke 21:1-4).

(ii) *How should I give?* Generously (2 Cor. 8:2; Mark 12:43-44), cheerfully (2 Cor. 9:7), regularly (1 Cor. 16:1), and privately (2 Cor. 9:7; Matt. 6:1-4).

(iii) *What amount should I give?* "Each according to his ability", "as he may prosper", "according to what one has" (Acts 11:29; 1 Cor. 16:2; 2 Cor. 8:12). If the people of God in the Old Testament times could give more than 10% of their income and yet survived, can we today give less (Lev. 27:30-33; Deut. 12:17-18; Ex. 25)? The problem with many is that they do not live within their means. We should be aiming to give a minimum of 10% of our gross income. To some, "each according to his ability" may mean 40% or even 60%!

9.3   Some Concluding Remarks

1 There is a vital connection between the spirituality of a congregation and the offerings received each week (Prov. 3:9-10; 2 Cor. 8:3-5). In the Old Testament, every time there was reformation and revival, tithing was re-introduced (2 Chron. 31; Neh. 10-13; Mal. 3). Generous giving will lead to abundant blessings (Mal. 3:10-12; 2 Cor. 9:8-11).

2 God's people had, in the past, said, "The time has not come, the time that the Lord's house should be built." God's answer was, "Is it time for you yourselves to dwell in your paneled houses, and this temple to lie in ruins (Hag. 1:2-4)?" Can this charge be levelled at us today?

3 As a church we should make it our deliberate policy to be self-supporting from the start, without relying on foreign aid. Otherwise, the next generation of believers will have a "dependent men-

tality" which will sap our spiritual vitality. If anything, we should be giving to more needy churches in other parts of the world.

4 Gospel work should be supported by givings from church members, not by businesses conducted by the church. The church has only one mandate from God, namely to uphold and propagate the truth, thereby glorifying God and building up the church (Phil. 2:16; Matt. 28:18-20; Eph. 3:21; 5:25-27). Just as the preacher should not be entangled with the affairs of this life (2 Tim. 2:4), so also the church.

Questions

1 Does 1 Timothy 5:17 permit the support of only preachers (cf. 1 Tim. 5:3-4, 16)? Is it beneficial to support workers of other kinds in the church?

2 In what practical ways may church members help in the livelihood of the pastor and his family (Gal. 6:6)?

3 Church members should support the ministry by prayer, submission, and finance. How does: (a) fear of God's judgement (Ps. 44:21; Joshua 7:10ff.) and, (b) belief in His promises (Mal. 3:10-12; Matt. 6:25-34) and, (c) love for God (Luke 7:47; 2 Cor. 5:14-15), motivate us in these?

Ten

Church Government (Matt. 18:15-20; Rev. 1:9-20)

Organisations, clubs and societies need some form of government, or administration, to function well. God has ordained three basic institutions in the world – the nation, the family, and the church. The church, whether considered as a whole (the universal church) or as a congregation (the local church), is the body of Christ (1 Cor. 12:12-13). Since Christ is the head of the church, and acts as a king (Eph. 5:23; 1 Tim. 6:15; Rev. 19:16), we would expect to find sufficient and clear teaching in the Bible on how the local church is to be governed.

10.1   Basic Principles Of Church Government

1 *The headship of Christ:* Jesus Christ is alone the head of the church (Col. 1:18; Eph. 5:23). He has given to each local church all the power needed to govern itself (Matt. 18:15-17). This being the case, the following are true:

(i) *Independent:* This concerns the form of the church. There should be no denominationalism, i.e. the situation in which a group of churches are bound together by a common government. Put in a different way, we believe that churches should be independent of one another, and be self-ruling. We, therefore, reject the systems practised by the Church of England and Presbyterian denominations, in which there is an hierarchy of individuals or committees of individuals who rule over a number of churches. Churches may associate together in fellowship, but not in government. In Revelation 1-3, the lampstands (which represent local churches) are separate from one another and not joined. Christ is present in their midst, to show that their unity is spiritual in nature, and not organisational.

(ii) *Autonomous:* This concerns the practice of the church. The local church is self-ruling. There should be no interference from any authority, whether ecclesiastical or civil, from outside the church. A church may seek counsel and help from others, but it should not allow itself to be controlled by any individual or committee of individuals from outside the church. Interference by the civil authority should also not be allowed. Christians should be the most law-abiding citizens in the country, but they should not allow their faith and the internal affairs of the church to be interfered with by the civil authorities.

(iii) *Communion of churches:* Churches may voluntarily associate together as a grouping for mutual edification and in gospel work (Gal. 1:2; Rev. 1:20), without compromising the independence and autonomy of the member churches.

2 *Rule by elders:* The power which Christ has given to the church is meant to be exercised by elders.

(i) There are only two offices appointed for the New Testament churches – those of elder and deacon (1 Tim. 3:8-13; Phil. 1:1). The words "elders" and "overseers" are used interchangeably (Acts 20:17, 28; Phil. 1:1). The extraordinary offices of apostle, prophet, and evangelist were withdrawn once the foundation of the church was laid, by the completion of the revelation of Jesus Christ (1 Cor. 3:11; Eph. 2:20). The apostles were given the ability to perform signs, wonders and miracles for two basic reasons:

(a) to confirm that they were true messengers of Christ (Mark 16:17-18, 20; 2 Cor. 12:12); and

(b) to confirm that the message they were preaching truly came from Christ (Heb. 2:3-4). The prophets and evangelists were able to perform signs, wonders and miracles for the same reasons (Acts 21:8 cf. 8:5-6; 6:8).

(ii) Of the two types of office-bearers, only the elders have the power to rule the church. The work of ruling or governing the flock is specifically entrusted to them (Acts 20:28; 1 Tim. 3:5; 1 Pet. 5:2). Church members must submit to them, by obeying them and respecting them (Heb. 13:7, 17; 1 Thess. 5:12). Deacons do not have power to rule. Their task is to take care of the outward, temporal, concerns of the church. This is clear from the example in Acts 6:1, and from the fact that the Greek word *diakonos* means a servant (Matt. 20:26; Mark 9:35; Rom. 15:8, etc.).

(iii) From 1 Timothy 5:17-18, we learn that there are two sorts of elders – those who rule and teach (called "teaching elders", for convenience), and those who only rule (called "ruling elders" for convenience). The teaching elders are also called "pastors" because they feed the flock by the word (Eph. 4:11-15; Jer. 3:15). They are also known as "ministers" because they serve the Lord by bringing His word to people (1 Cor. 3:5; 2 Cor. 3:6; 6:4; 11:23; 1 Tim. 4:6; etc.).

(iv) The elders rule the church together as a body (Acts 20:17, 28; 1 Tim. 5:17). Under the guidance of the pastor (or one of them, if there are more than one pastor), the elders make the decisions for the church. The congregation does not have the authority to rule the church, whether by democratic voting or through an executive committee.

3 *Congregational consent:* The decisions made by the elders for the church cannot be implemented unless the congregation gives its consent or agreement. The authority of the elders extend over two areas: teaching and administration. These have been called "the key of teaching (or order)" and "the key of administration (or jurisdiction)", based on Matthew 16:19 and 18:18. In the area of teaching, which covers the public proclamation of God's word and the application of God's word in private admonition, the consent was given at the appointment of the elders. In the area of administration, which covers decisions that affect the external circumstances of the whole church, consent is given by a show of hands or by secret ballot during a church business meeting. Rule with congregational consent may be proven from apostolic examples:

(i) The appointment of elders and deacons involved congregational consent (Acts 1:15-26; 6:1-7; 14:21-23).

(ii) The congregation was also involved in the appointment of delegates of churches (Acts 15:1-3; 1 Cor. 16:3; 2 Cor. 8:19).

(iii) In the settlement of disputes, the elders made the decisions with congregational consent (Acts 15:6; 16:4 cf. 15:22, 23, 25).

(iv) The congregation was involved in the exercise of church discipline (1 Cor. 5:4-5, 7).

10.2   Some Relevant Comments

1 In the government of the church, there is always the danger of authoritarianism, i.e. high-handedness in dealing with individuals. Elders are to take care of the members in the spirit of a shepherd who takes care of the flock (John 10:11-18; 1 Pet. 5:2-4). They are to rule with the aim of edifying the church and glorifying Christ. They must be careful not to engage in "heavy shepherding", i.e. close pastoral care that intrudes into the legitimate liberties of the members.

2 We have considered three main principles of church government. There are other related principles which, together with these, define for us the biblical *form*, or system, of church government. That form has been called "Independency", in contradistinction to Episcopacy, Presbyterianism and Congregationalism. (See Poh, 1997; Poh, 2017).

3 Form without substance is useless, but substance without form is potentially dangerous. We must ensure that we have the biblical way of ruling the church (the form), without compromising on doctrine (the substance). Having form and substance is still not good enough. We must ensure that there is spiritual life in the church. How we must remain humble, teachable and faithful as a church!

Questions

1 Jesus Christ, as head of the church, acts as prophet, priest and king. The church ought to respond to His offices of prophet, priest and king by having correct doctrine, pure worship and a right form of church government. Discuss the relative importance of doctrine, worship and church government.

2 Is an unmarried man disqualified from the office of elder (cf. 1 Tim. 3:2)? How may we determine whether he is suitable to be an elder? Would there be areas of service that an unmarried elder cannot discharge?

3 Some churches have deaconesses, women elders, and even women pastors. Discuss whether this is right (1 Tim. 3:11 cf. Rom. 16:1; 1 Cor. 11:1-16; 1 Tim. 2:12-15; 3:1-13). Consider the value of having women actively involved in gospel work (1 Cor. 14:33-35; 11:7-16; 1 Tim. 2:12 cf. 1 Cor. 11:5; Acts 1:14; Rom. 16:7ff.; Phil. 4:3; 1 Cor. 9:5; 1 Tim. 5:9-10; Tit. 2:3-5).

References

1 Poh, Boon-Sing, 1997. Independency: The Biblical Form Of Church Government. Good News Enterprise.

2 Poh, Boon-Sing. The Keys Of The Kingdom: A Study On The Biblical Form Of Church Government. Good News Enterprise.

Eleven

Church Discipline (1 Cor. 5:1-12)

C hurch discipline is a broad subject which encompasses the whole of church government. A narrower definition would cover that area of church life which deals with the nurturing and preservation of the spiritual life of the members. There are three aspects to such church discipline:

 i *Formative:* This covers the efforts involved in forming the character of the Christians so that they are transformed more and more by the truths of Scripture (Rom. 121-7).

 ii *Preventive:* This covers the means by which church members are prevented from falling into sins and spiritual decay, including attending to "the means of grace" (hearing preaching, prayer, service, fellowship, the Lord's Supper, etc.), pastoral oversight, reaffirmation of the church covenant, etc. (Heb. 10:24-25; 13:7, 17).

iii *Corrective:* This refers to efforts to restore members who sin in life and doctrine (1 Cor. 5:11; Rom. 16:17; Tit. 3:10).

Our concern is with corrective discipline.

11.1   Corrective Discipline

1 *Objections:* In many churches, corrective discipline is most needed but least practised. Reasons given include the following:

(i) The need to preserve peace, and that we are not to "rock the boat";

(ii) To prevent scandal in the eyes of the world;

(iii) It is unloving;

(iv) It is open to the abuse of authoritarianism, in which the person being disciplined is crushed by high-handedness on the part of the elders.

These reasons are invalid because:

(i) Greater problems will arise when the initial problems are not dealt with;

(ii) Scandals are more likely, and more damaging, when the sins become fully-blown;

(iii) Faithfulness to God and love for souls require that discipline be exercised;

(iv) The danger of authoritarianism does not justify laxity and toleration of sins.

2 *Procedures:*

(i) In private disputes, the steps delineated in Matthew 18:15-17 arc to be followed. Problems often arise because the biblical procedures are not observed. Instead of telling the offending brother his fault, the offended person goes around telling others. A word of caution, however, is needed. Over-sensitive souls may read too much into the actions of others and form negative conclusions about their intentions. It would be wise for them to ensure that there is just cause for taking offence before following the steps of Matthew 18:15-17. Often it is that "love will cover a multitude of sins" (1 Pet. 4:8). In other words, a forgiving spirit will prevent minor incidents from developing into all kinds of offences.

(ii) In public sins, or unsettled private disputes, the elders are to determine the truth of the matter. If there is irrefutable proof, the steps needed to restore the sinning brother are as follows:

> (a) *Admonition*, i.e. correcting and rebuking as necessary (Tit. 3:10);
>
> (b) *Suspension*, i.e. the withdrawal of the privileges of church membership (2 Thess. 3:6-15); and,
>
> (c) *Excommunication*, i.e. the removal of the person from the membership of the church, and treating him henceforth as an unbeliever (1 Cor. 5; Matt. 18:17).

3 *Scope and spirit of discipline:*

(i) Corrective discipline applies to sins of conduct or doctrine, and neglect of membership responsibilities. It cannot be applied to sins of the heart, e.g. dishonesty, selfishness, sinful intentions, etc., until those sins are manifested. The elders of the church may need to take precautionary actions to prevent sins being committed, but those would fall into the categories of formative and preventive disciplines.

(ii) Corrective discipline is to be carried out with meekness – involving gentleness, humility and carefulness (Gal. 6:1) – with the aim of restoring the sinning brother (2 Cor. 10:8). Some may need a harsh rebuke, while others may need a milder treatment (Jude 22).

11.2   Some Concluding Comments

1 Churches tend to be too lax or too strict in the implementation of discipline. Lack of understanding in this area has resulted in churches being thrown into confusion when a case of discipline arises.

2 Corrective discipline is necessary because of our concern for:

(i) *God's glory:* God is holy and will not tolerate sin. The church should reflect the holy character of God. Remember Achan (Joshua 7), and the Lord's warning to the churches in Asia (Rev. 2:5, 14ff.).

(ii) *The purity of Christ's church:* Just as individual believers must grow in holiness, so must the local church. That way, we will be preparing ourselves for heaven (Eph. 5:25-27).

(iii) *The good of men's souls:* It is the God-appointed way to restore a sinner. It has a sobering effect, reminding other believers to walk carefully before God (Acts 5:11; 1 Tim. 5:20). Note that the deterrent effect is only an incidental benefit. The aim of church discipline should primarily be to restore the sinner.

Questions

1 Church leaders may not see the need to exercise corrective discipline, as happened in 1 Corinthians 5. What may church members do to correct the situation?

2 Diotrephes was a church leader who wrongly used church discipline to eliminate opposition (3 John 9-11). What are the differences between egocentric (proud and self-centred) lust for power and zeal for the gospel? What may church members do when there is such abuse of power in the church?

3 It is always a painful thing to have to implement corrective discipline. When such a situation arises, how may: (a) church leaders help the church members, and (b) church members help the leaders?

Twelve

Church Membership
(Heb. 8:1-13)

Although convinced of the importance of the local church, many people remain unsure whether there should be such a thing as church membership. A combination of reasons account for this:

i They somehow think that the church, being a spiritual organisation, should not be the same as the clubs and societies in the world. In their mind, the church is a place of worship to which anyone can go when he feels like it.

ii The sacral churches, such as the Roman Catholic Church and the Anglican Church, have contributed to this way of thinking. They believe in a territorial concept of the church, in which everyone born in a certain area, called a "parish", belongs to the church there. Church membership is, therefore, related to the place of birth or residence, without any commitment on the part of the people.

iii Many churches today practise a loose concept of church membership. Others, such as the Brethren churches, do not believe that there should be an explicit (definite, clearly defined) membership. A believer who comes regularly to the meetings of the church is automatically regarded as a "member".

Church membership is in fact a teaching of the Bible. It flows from the concept of the church covenant. What is the church covenant?

12.1   The Church Covenant

1 *The Covenant of Redemption:* God deals with His people by covenant. From eternity, the three persons of the Holy Trinity had agreed to save certain people from their sins (Eph. 1:3-14; 2 Thess. 2:13; 2 Tim. 1:9; etc.). God the Father agreed to give to His Son a people. The Son of God agreed to come and die for them. The Holy Spirit agreed to apply the work of Christ savingly to these people. In theology, this is called "the Covenant of Redemption" or "the Eternal Covenant".

2 *The Covenant of Grace:* The Covenant of Redemption works itself out in history as "the Covenant of Grace". The main promise in the covenant, which includes all the other promises, is contained in the words, "I will be their God, and they shall be My people." By this covenant, God binds Himself to save His people through the work of Jesus Christ. The covenant is expressed, or manifested, in different ways in history. The different manifestations of the covenant in the Old Testament culminated in "the Mosaic Covenant" in which God dealt with His people as a nation. This is also known as "the old covenant", in contrast to "the new

covenant" that was brought into effect by the coming of Christ (Heb. 8:6, 7, 13).

3 *The form of the church:* The Covenant of Grace is essentially one covenant. The Old Testament believers were saved by faith in the coming Saviour, while the New Testament believers are saved by faith in the Saviour who has come (Heb. 4:2; 1 Cor. 10:1-3; Gal. 3:8). God saves people *individually,* to be a member of the *community* of His people (Matt. 28:18-20; 1 Cor. 12). Put another way, the *manner* of salvation is individualistic and the *end* of salvation is communal. The primary parties in the Covenant of Grace are God and His people. In any covenant, e.g. marriage, there must be a response, or agreement, to the terms of the covenant by all the parties involved. In the Old Testament, God's people responded as a nation to the terms of His covenant (Ex. 24:1-8; Dt. 29:10-15; Ezra 10:3-5; Neh. 9:1-3, 38; 10:1; etc.). Although not explicitly stated, the New Testament communities of God's people, i.e. the local churches, would have responded to the terms of the Covenant of Grace. See 2 Corinthians 6:16-18 and Hebrews 8:10 (cf. Ezek. 37:26-27), in which the promise of the covenant is applied to believers of the New Testament. The response of believers as a community, or local church, to the Covenant of Grace is what we call "the covenant of the church". Membership in the covenant community is therefore explicit, i.e. clearly defined. This was so in the Old Testament time, and this should be true also in local churches today.

4 *The matter of the church:* The discontinuity of the Old and New Testaments, of the old and new covenants, is also emphasised in the Bible (Heb. 8:6, 7, 13; Matt. 9:16-17). The continuity of the Testaments gives rise to the form of the church, while the disconti-

nuity gives rise to the matter. In the old covenant, the members of the covenant community were Israelites. Non-Israelites, e.g. Ruth, had to be absorbed into the nation to enjoy the covenant privileges. Only some were regenerate (1 Cor. 10:1-5; Heb. 3:15-17). In the new covenant, membership in the covenant community is defined spiritually. All the members, without exception, must be believers (Heb. 8:10-12). Although we do not ultimately know whether a person is saved or not, we are to exercise discretion and accept into membership only those with a *credible profession of faith*.

5 *The covenanted community:* It is with this understanding of the form and matter of the church that many of the New Testament passages make sense, e.g. Acts 2:41-42; 1 Corinthians 5:4-5, 12-13; 14:23-24. These conclusions follow:

(i) A new church is formed by conducting a covenanting service. This is like a normal worship service in which there are hymns, Scripture reading, preaching, and prayer. The main purpose of the occasion, however, is the covenanting together of those who are forming the membership. In the midst at the service, these individuals would stand and raise their right hand to read the church covenant aloud together, led by the appointed man. This is a vow made to God, and witnessed by others present. As such, it should not be taken lightly, just as one would not take the marriage vow lightly. They then affix their signatures to the membership book, in which a copy of the church covenant is pasted. The Lord's Supper, for the members alone on this occasion, follows.

(ii) The members should all have been baptised prior to this occasion. All who are accepted into the membership of the church subsequently should also be baptised. Baptism is a pre-requisite of membership with the local church, just as regeneration is a prerequisite of membership with the universal church. This is shown in the diagram of Fig. 12.1.[1]

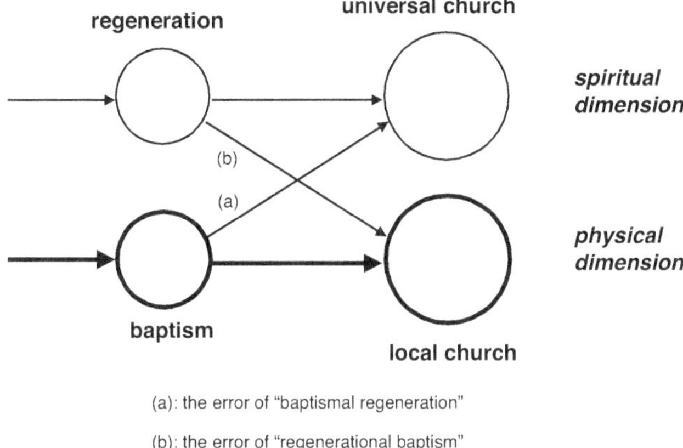

Fig. 12.1: Relationship between Regeneration and Baptism

(iii) The local church should adopt one of the historic Confessions of Faith as its doctrinal basis. That is because, as a covenanted community, we wish to declare what we believe. The Bible is the only authority of faith and practice. Just as we are not ashamed to declare verbally our beliefs, so also we are not ashamed to de-

---

[1]The physical dimension is a reflection of the spiritual dimension. The universal church is manifested in the world as local churches. Regeneration, which is invisible, is shown visibly by baptism.

Some churches teach the error of "baptismal regeneration", i.e. that baptism saves, or is necessary to salvation.

Just as there is the error of "baptismal regeneration", we may say there is the error of "regenerational baptism", i.e. the idea that anyone who is regenerate should be considered a member of the local church, regardless of whether or not he is baptised. The paedobaptists teaches "regenerational baptism" of another kind, in which infants born to believers are baptised into membership of the church on presumed regeneration. In the one case, baptism is waived because of regeneration, in the other case baptism is given on presumed regeneration.

clare them in writing. When that is done, we have effectively a Confession of Faith! We do not wish to "re-invent the wheel". We, therefore, adopt the 1689 Baptist Confession of Faith as a concise, yet sufficiently full, declaration of the faith of the church.

12.2   Responsibilities Of Church Membership

1 *Submission:*

(i) To biblical oversight (Heb. 13:17; 1 Thess. 5:12).

(ii) To God's word, as it is expounded in church.

2 *Support:*

(i) *Attendance:* Meetings are kept to a minimum while attendance is expected to be at a maximum. Sunday worship, prayer meetings, Bible Studies, and church business meetings, ought to be complete family gatherings. Every absentee is missed every time!

(ii) *Givings:* Money is needed to support the ministry, maintain the church building, send forth missionaries, buy necessary equipment and teaching aids, and care for the sick and needy. If members do not give, who else will?

(iii) *Prayer:* The pastor, every department of gospel work, and the general welfare of the church must be prayed for.

3 *Service:*

(i) *Fellowship:* Every member has something to contribute to the welfare of the church. Every member should feel that he or she belongs. There should be love for one another, despite individual faults (Rom. 5:8; John 15:12).

(ii) *Soul-winning:* This can be properly accomplished only by all working in fellowship.

12.3   Concluding Points

1 Many Christians refuse to become members of a local church for various reasons:

(i) Ignorance of this teaching, that there is such a thing as church membership;

(ii) Lack of submissiveness to rightful authority, in this case, to spiritual oversight;

(iii) Fear of the responsibilities of membership, not knowing that the Lord expects only what we are able to do;

(iv) Disillusioned with the many dead, half-dead, unfaithful, or authoritarian churches around.

2 Christ, through His church, has the highest claim upon you (Matt. 10:37-38; 1 Sam. 2:30). If you are not a member of any church yet, it is time to join one. No church is perfect, but make sure that you join one which is attempting to preach and live up to God's word faithfully.

Questions

1 Suppose a "famous" preacher comes to preach in town. Would you go to the meeting if it clashes with your own church meeting? A friend visits you when you wish to attend the Bible Study. Would you stay back to entertain him, or would you go to the Bible Study?

2 A Christian comes to study at the university. There are evangelical churches nearby, but he prefers to go to a church of his denomination some twenty miles away despite difficulties of transport. What can you say to this? What if it is a family man, and he has his own car?

3 You are transferred to a town where: (a) there is no Reformed church of any kind; (b) there is no Evangelical church of any kind. What would you do?

Thirteen

Our Aim In Life (Eph. 1:3-14; 3:8-21)

This study completes our series on the local church. Much more may be said, but a stop has to be made somewhere.

The life of a local church is linked to God's plan of redemption. It is also linked to the life of the individual believer. One's life on earth is of limited span. We would want to live usefully for God. It will be good, therefore, to stand back and consider our aim in life.

13.1   Some Concluding Points

1 *In relation to God's plan of redemption:* God's plan of redeeming for Himself a people works out in history in a definite and progressive way – along the godly line of descent from Adam through Abel, Seth, Noah, Shem, Abraham, the remnant within the nation of Israel, believers during and after is the time of Christ. These constitute the "invisible church". The "visible church" was manifested as the patriarchal families, the nation of Israel, and finally,

New Testament congregations. The glorious plan of redemption in Christ is described in Ephesians 1-3. Ephesians 3:21 is significant. Life is without purpose if not seen in the light of God's plan of redemption.

2 *In relation to God's purpose for the local church:* Salvation is not to be viewed only from the personal aspect. There is also a communal aspect to it. As believers are sanctified, the local churches are sanctified. As local churches are sanctified, the church universal is sanctified (Eph. 5:25-27). The local church is central and unique in the purposes of God. It is a multifaceted jewel. Church membership is a biblical duty. We must live to build up the local church, and thereby build up the universal church, and glorify Christ. Many people talk about building up the universal church of Christ but contribute nothing of significance towards that because they do not build up their own local churches.

3 *In relation to the objective of the local church:* As a church, we should concentrate on planting other gospel churches. Our aim is not to have mere numbers, but to extend the kingdom of God and thereby bring glory to His name. Towards this end:

(i) *Churches:* We establish congregations wherever possible, and viable. Gospel proclamation and soul-winning are involved. We concentrate on people, not buildings (Matt. 28:19-20; Rom. 10:14-15).

(ii) *Members:* We build up church members. Teaching and nurturing are involved (Eph. 4:11-16; 2 Tim. 3:16-17).

(iii) *Preachers:* We pray for, train up, and send out preachers and church planters (2 Tim. 2:2; Heb. 5:12).

(iv) *Interchurch fellowship:* Maintain close fellowship with like-minded churches, and wider fellowship with other Evangelical churches, to further the wider cause of Christ (Eph. 4:1-4). Consider your role, know your place in the church, and contribute towards achieving the objective of the church. See Fig. 13.1.

4 *In relation to the type of church we wish to found:* We need to balance between striving for the ideal and yet remaining realistic. We wish to maintain our distinctives because each church is answerable to the Lord (Rev. 2 & 3). We wish to maintain fellowship with other churches wherever and whenever possible (Eph. 4:1-6). All biblical truths must be held in balance and proportion.

(i) The doctrine of God is important because it is of the essence of the Christian faith.

(ii) The doctrine of Scripture is important because it is the basis of faith.

(iii) The doctrine of salvation is important because it is of the essence of the gospel.

(iv) The doctrine of the church is important because it affects our intention to found gospel churches.

We wish to be known in this order of importance – Christian, Evangelical, Reformed, Baptist. That is best achieved only when we work in the reverse order. Compare this with the fulfilment of the Great Commission – beginning from Jerusalem, to all Judea and Samaria, and to the end of the earth (Acts 1:8). See Fig. 13.1.

5 *In relation to the identity of our church(es):* How should we name our churches? A name should identify ourselves. Otherwise, there is no reason for calling ourselves anything. It should tell people who we are, what we believe, what we are like. Until such time as

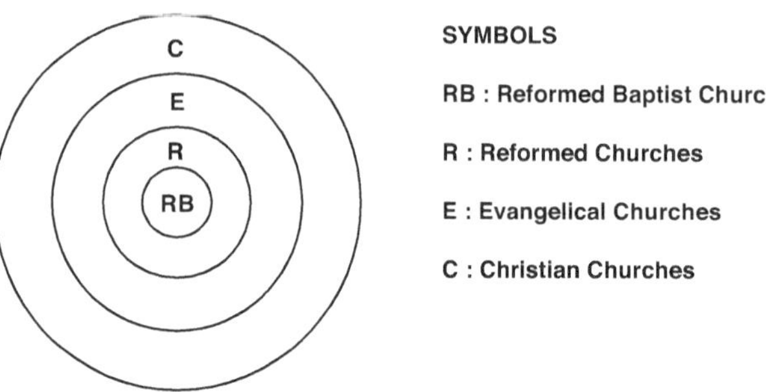

Fig. 13.1: Degree of Fellowship with Other Churches

the term becomes distorted, "Reformed Baptist" may be used for the following reasons:

(i) It describes us as what we wish to be known – Evangelical, Reformed (or Calvinist), and Baptist. Should we be ashamed of the truths which we believe to be biblical?

(ii) It is helpful to people of like convictions who are looking for a church to join or worship in.

(iii) It is being honest to others of different convictions as they seek to fellowship with us or to avoid us.

(iv) It is appropriate from the historical and doctrinal points of view.[1]

Baptists have historically been most consistent and thorough in maintaining:

---

[1] See Poh, 2017, What Is A Reformed Baptist Church?

(a) the authority of Scripture, by which all doctrine and practice must be tested;

(b) the true nature of discipleship, in which religious liberty and the rights of conscience are upheld; and

(c) the purity of the church, in which only those with credible professions of faith are admitted into church membership, and church discipline is observed.

We are Reformed because:

(a) The Particular Baptists, with whom we identify, arose directly out of the Reformation;

(b) We hold to the main truths and emphases recovered during the Reformation; and

(c) We share the same reforming spirit as the Reformers (whether Magisterial or Radical)[1] of desiring to be biblical and God-honouring in doctrine and practice.

6 *In relation to the ultimate purpose of man:* What is the chief end of man? Man's chief end is to glorify God, and to enjoy Him for ever.[2]

(i) To enjoy God, we must live to glorify His name (Eph. 1:6; 1 Cor. 10:31).

(ii) To glorify His name, we must live to glorify His Son (John 5:23; Rom. 8:29; 15:3; Phil. 2:5; John 13:15).

(iii) To glorify His Son, we must live in righteousness and holiness (Eph. 1:4; 4:20-24).

(iv) The whole purpose of living in righteousness and in holiness is that the church of Christ may be built up (Eph. 2:19-22; 4:16)

---

[2]Shorter Catechism & Keach's Catechism, Q. 1.

(v) The universal church of Christ is built up when local churches are built up numerically and spiritually (Matt. 28:19-20; Eph. 5:25-27; 1 Cor. 9:24-27 cf. 19-23).

(vi) It follows that to fulfill the chief end of man, a person should live to build up local churches!

Questions

1 What possible dangers or disadvantages are there in calling ourselves "Reformed Baptist"? Does a "neutral" name solve the problem?

2 Can we fulfill man's chief end without being consciously involved in building up local churches? What difference would it make if one lives consciously to do so?

3 Do you agree that the local church is "a multifaceted jewel"? How has this series of studies contributed to your understanding of the local church? What are the most striking things you have learned? How should they affect your life?

References

1 Poh, Boon-Sing. 2017. What Is A Reformed Baptist Church? Good News Enterprise.

2 Keach's Catechism, produced by the Particular Baptists of the 17th century, and used by the Reformed Baptists today.

3 The Shorter Catechism, produced by the Presbyterians of the 17th century, and used by many Presbyterian churches today.

✤ ✤ ✤ ✤ ✤

DOCTRINAL STATEMENT

POLITY

And

COVENANT

Of

XYZ REFORMED BAPTIST CHURCH

INTRODUCTION

This Constitution consists of three parts – the Doctrinal Statement, the Polity, and the Covenant of Members – of XYZ Reformed Baptist Church. It is adopted on this day of (Date Month Year) when the church is constituted. The Comments are not to be understood as substance of the Constitution but as clarification of the substance. While the Comments may be omitted or altered, the substance of the Constitution may not be altered except under the conditions specified in Article 34 of the Polity.

DOCTRINAL STATEMENT

We express our agreement with the London Baptist Confession of Faith of 1689.[1] We further draw particular attention to the following truths:

1. THE BIBLE: THE WORD OF GOD

The inerrancy and infallibility of the Holy Scriptures as originally given; their verbal inspiration by God; their authority and all-sufficiency, as not only containing, but being in themselves, the word of God; the reliability of the New Testament in its testimony to the character and authorship of the Old Testament; and the need of the teaching of the Holy Spirit for a true and spiritual understanding of the whole. The Holy Scriptures constitute our only standard of faith and rule of conduct, and are the sixty-six books of the Old and New Testaments as contained in the Table of Contents of the 1982 New King James Version.

2. THE FATHER, THE SON, THE HOLY SPIRIT : ONE GOD

The Trinity of the Godhead as revealed in the Scriptures – the Father being God, the Lord Jesus Christ the Son being God, the Holy Spirit being God, these being equal in power and glory, one Lord God Almighty – sovereign in creation, providence and redemption.

3. JESUS CHRIST: TRUE GOD, TRUE MAN

---

[1]The Reformed Baptist Churches in Malaysia have the following included, "the clause in Chapter 26, Article 4, which equates the pope with the man of sin, excepted." There is no disagreement over the facts that the Roman Catholic Church is apostate and the pope is an antichrist. They have historically been the instrument of Satan in repressing truth and the killing of many faithful believers. It is believed, however, from an exegetical point of view, that 2 Thessalonians 2:2-9 is a reference to a far more subtle, powerful, and dangerous man than the pope or the Roman Catholic Church.

The essential, absolute and eternal deity of the Lord Jesus Christ; His conception by the Holy Spirit; His birth of the virgin Mary; His real but sinless humanity; the authority of His teaching, and the infallibility of all His utterances; His voluntary humiliation in life as a Man of Sorrows, culminating in His substitutionary and atoning death whereby He shed His precious blood as the sacrifice for sin; His bodily resurrection on the third day; His ascension into heaven as the only eternal Mediator between God and man; His present High Priestly intercession for His people at the right hand of the Father; and His personal return in power and glory.

4. THE HOLY SPIRIT: AUTHOR AND GIVER OF LIFE

The personality and the deity of the Holy Spirit, who inspired holy men to write the Scriptures, authenticating their writing and ministry by means of supernatural gifts which He has since withdrawn. Through Him alone the soul is born again to saving repentance and faith, and by Him the saints are sanctified through the truth. The necessity for His work in ministry and worship.

5. FALLEN MAN: A SINNER

The universal and total depravity of man in the sight of God as a consequence of the fall; his exposure to everlasting punishment; his inability to will any spiritual good accompanying salvation and therefore the necessity for regeneration.

6. SALVATION: BY GRACE THROUGH FAITH

The justification of the sinner for ever; by grace; through faith; through the atoning merits of our Lord Jesus Christ, whose righteousness imputed to him is the only ground of acceptance before God.

7. HOLINESS & WITNESS: EVIDENCE OF CONVERSION

A holy walk and life on the part of professed believers as the evidence of their conversion to God. It is the duty of every Christian and every church of Christ to seek to extend His gospel to the ends of the earth. This is to be done by personal effort and by all other methods sanctioned by the word of God.

8. OUR LORD'S ORDINANCES: BAPTISM & HIS TABLE

The ordinances of baptism and the Lord's table as instituted by our Lord Jesus Christ. Baptism is the total immersion in water, in the Triune Name, of those who have professed repentance toward God and faith in the Lord Jesus Christ. The Lord's table is in no sense a sacrifice for sin, and involves no change in the substance of the bread and wine.

9. THE FUTURE: HEAVEN AND HELL

The resurrection of the body; the judgment of the world by our Lord Jesus Christ, with the everlasting blessedness of the saved, and the everlasting punishment of the wicked.

10. THE ONE CHURCH: CALLED TO BE PURE

The spiritual unity of all who truly believe in the Lord Jesus Christ, and their duty to maintain in themselves and in the church a standard of life and doctrine that is in conformity with the teaching of God's word.

****

POLITY

THIS CHURCH RECOGNISES THE LORD JESUS CHRIST AS ITS SUPREME HEAD, and undertakes to manage its own affairs according to the word of God, and seeks under the guidance of the Holy Spirit and according to Holy Scripture to be "reformed" and "non-charismatic" both in teaching and practice.

A. ORDINANCES

1. The ordinance of believer's baptism by immersion shall be observed as and when required. Candidates shall be examined by two elders before being baptised, and shall receive a copy of this Constitution and other literature pertaining to baptism and church membership. They shall, upon baptism, be received into membership of this church. Under extraordinary circumstances, candidates who have been examined by two elders may be baptised with the understanding that they shall associate themselves with a visible body of believers elsewhere.

2. The ordinance of the Lord's Supper shall be observed regularly. Although we maintain that the ordinances should be observed in the scriptural order, the table shall be open to all believers in the Lord Jesus Christ who are walking orderly.

[Comments: Those who are under disciplinary measures in their churches should not be allowed to partake in the Lord's Supper.]

B. PASTOR

3. The status of a pastor is that he is an elder of the local flock sharing its oversight with other elders. He is set aside by the congregation to

give himself more fully to labouring in the word and doctrine, and to lead the eldership. If there are more than one pastors, one of them shall be recognised as the leading elder.

[Comments: When no pastor has been appointed, the elders should choose one from among themselves to be the leading elder. This choice should be ratified by the members at a church members' meeting.]

4. The pastorate shall be held only by such men as believe and uphold the truths set down in the doctrinal standards of the church.

5. The pastor shall have the oversight, with the other elders, over all departments of ministry in the church. He normally presides over the meetings of the elders, the court of office bearers, and the church members' meetings.

[Comments: Practically, a minimum of a pastor and an elder is needed to form an eldership, or presbytery (1 Tim. 5:17 cf. 4:14; 2 Tim. 1:6). Any less can hardly constitute an eldership. We believe in the principles of "rule by elders", "the priority of the ministry", "the validity of ruling elders", and "the unity of the eldership".]

C. OFFICE-BEARERS

6. The full court of office-bearers shall consist of three elders and three deacons, though this number may be varied to serve the current needs of the church. They shall be male members of the church, possessing the scriptural qualifications (1 Tim. 3:1-13; Tit. 1:5-9), and who have been duly appointed. Two of the office-bearers, preferably elders, shall be the Secretary and the Treasurer, respectively.

[Comments: Some elders are not good at handling the duties of Secretary or Treasurer, in which case the deacons may be appointed to these posts. The duties of the Secretary include recording minutes, mak-

ing announcements, updating the membership roll, corresponding with other churches when directed by the elders' court or pastor, and keeping a diary of the church. The Treasurer has no power to make unilateral decisions on the finances of the church. He carries out his duties under the oversight of the elders.]

7. An elder or a deacon shall remain in office for as long as he possesses the scriptural qualifications and is functioning as an elder or deacon, respectively. Any lapse on the part of an office-bearer shall be dealt with within the court of office-bearers. Any recommendation for removal, or application for resignation, from office shall be made known to the church at a members' meeting. It shall be effected by ballot, with a two-thirds majority of those present, at a subsequent church members' meeting.

8. The office-bearers shall have the management of the finances of the church. The elders shall concentrate on those matters pertaining to the spiritual welfare of the fellowship. The deacons shall concentrate on the management and care of the properties, meetings, and benevolent works. The elders shall meet at least once a month, and together with the deacons as circumstances may require. At all such meetings, half shall form a quorum. When an insufficient number of elders have been appointed to constitute the elders' court, other men in the church may be called upon by the pastor or leading elder to sit in, and help in the deliberations of, the meeting.

[Comments: The expenditure of money is decided by the elders, in consultation with the deacons if necessary, without the need of congregational consent. Otherwise, the need for congregational consent over petty sums will adversely affect the running of the church. However, if large sums are involved, it is wise for the elders to get the consent

of the congregation. The office-bearers also decide on the pastor's pay, which is based on an accepted pay scheme. Otherwise, every time that a pay increment is discussed, the pastor's privacy is violated. The church members do not have their salaries paraded before their colleagues at their places of work!]

D. MEMBERSHIP

9. The membership of this church shall be composed of those who have professed repentance towards God and faith in our Lord Jesus Christ, and who have been immersed in the name of the Father, and of the Son, and of the Holy Spirit.

10. Any person desiring membership, but who has been baptised in another church, shall apply to one of the elders, and then shall receive a copy of this Constitution. Such application, if proceeded with, shall imply agreement with the Doctrinal Statement, acceptance of the Polity, willingness to submit to the biblical oversight of the elders, and readiness to enter into covenant with the church.

11. When such application is received, the candidate shall be nominated at the next church members' meeting. Two elders shall interview the candidate and their report shall be given at a subsequent meeting. The acceptance, or otherwise, of the candidate shall be decided by a majority of the members present.

12. Candidates accepted by the church shall be publicly received by the right hand of fellowship at the Lord's table. New members are required to sign the church register, thus completing the process of entering into covenant with the church.
[Comments: In covenanting together, the members vow to bind them-

selves as a body of Christ, to worship and serve God according to the terms and conditions spelt out in the Covenant. Like a marriage vow, it is a solemn undertaking that should not be lightly entered into.]

13. Those joining the membership of the church are earnestly reminded of the solemn responsibility involved in their union with the church, that henceforth they are responsible in their measure for its strength or weakness, its prosperity or decline. They are affectionately urged to pray daily for its welfare, that the Saviour may be glorified in the conversion of sinners to Himself, and in the consistent and blameless lives of those who have named His name. Unless providentially hindered, members are expected to attend the Sunday services and weekly prayer meeting, to be frequently at the Lord's table, and to engage in some Christian work in connection with the church. Leaders of church activities shall be members of the church who are approved by the elders. Those who may have been members of other churches before are reminded that henceforth their loyalty and commitment should be with this church.

[Comments: As a church, we keep meetings to a minimum and expect maximum attendance. Meetings are held for the good of the members and the advancement of the gospel. If members do not support these meetings, who else will? The attitude of the member will determine whether he attends all the meetings listed above, and other meetings organised by the church. It will also determine whether he attends the meetings punctually and joyfully. God is our Judge. See also point (c) of the Covenant.]

14. Scattered members, i.e. members removing to a distance which renders regular attendance impossible, shall openly associate with a visible body of believers in their area. They shall be expected to

communicate with the church through its elders at least once in six months, and if possible, to contribute to its funds.

15. A member who is no longer able to continue in this church without violating his conscience, or for any other good reason, may, as he thinks best, join himself to some other church after consulting with the elders of this church and receiving the approval of this church. Transfers of membership from one church to another should proceed in an orderly and gracious manner.

[Comments: If a member perceives that the church is sinning, in doctrine or practice, he may bring the matter before the elders for consideration and correction. If it is a case of strong disagreement with the doctrine, practice, or ministry of the church, that member should consider leaving amicably. Point (e) of the Covenant is pertinent.]

E. DISCIPLINE

16. We recognise three measures of corrective discipline: admonition, suspension and excommunication.

17. In all cases of private offence between members of the church it is incumbent that the rule prescribed by our Lord in Matthew 18:15-17 be faithfully observed.

18. In cases of open inconsistency it is the duty of the church to exercise discipline according to 2 Thessalonians 3:6-15. Such suspension shall be implemented by the eldership, and confirmed at the next church members' meeting.

19. Members under suspension shall be removed from all places of responsibility in the church, and excluded from participation in the

Lord's Supper, active participation in any other meeting, and attendance at church members' meetings.

20. In each case of suspension the elders, or members delegated by them, shall keep in touch with the suspended member.

21. Any member guilty of conduct deemed inconsistent with a Christian profession, or guilty of serious doctrinal error, may, by vote of the church, after due visitation and communication, be excluded from its fellowship (1 Cor. 5).

22. Similarly, any member absent from the Lord's table for twelve consecutive months without giving satisfactory reason when waited on or communicated with, may, by vote of the church, be removed from the membership roll.

23. There shall be an annual revision of the membership roll by the office-bearers' court, not later than the month of October, and recommendations arising therefrom shall be brought before the members for decision at a subsequent members' meeting.

24. All matters pertaining to church discipline shall be regarded as confidential within the church, and shall be conducted in the spirit of Galatians 6:1.

F. CHURCH MEMBERS' MEETINGS

25. A meeting of the church members shall be called by the elders when required. An oral notice of the meeting shall be given on the two Sundays preceding the meeting. All church members' meetings shall open and close with prayer.

26. Normal church members' meetings shall require fifty percent of the regular (i.e. unscattered) membership to form a quorum. Special church members' meetings (convened to elect a pastor, to amend the church constitution, or to dissolve the church) shall require three-quarters of the regular membership to form a quorum. Apart from procedural motions, which shall only require a simple majority, no resolution shall be considered as carried unless by a two-thirds majority of the members present.

27. Every church members' meeting shall be presided over by one of the elders (normally, the pastor), and such meeting shall not be continued for longer than two hours, unless by vote of the church then taken.

28. Members are invited to bring forward any matters relative to the welfare of the church. Normally, this is to be done by means of an oral request, or a letter, to the office-bearers' court, before a church members' meeting. It may also be done by means of an oral request at a members' meeting. Such new matter shall be deferred if a request for postponement is made by the office-bearers.

29. Pastor or pastors shall be chosen by ballot at a special members' meeting convened for that purpose. A two-thirds majority of those present shall be necessary to secure election. An oral notice of such meeting shall be given on the two preceding Lord's days.

30. When an election of elders (a pastor included) is necessary, the existing eldership shall nominate men who are suitable for the church's consideration. When an election of deacons is necessary, the

church meeting shall be reminded of the qualifications which Scripture requires of such officers (1 Tim. 3:8-13) and the duties which the church expects of them (cf. Acts 6:2, 3), and shall be requested to prayerfully seek out suitable men. Nomination of new deacon(s) by the church shall be submitted to the elders by a fixed date before the subsequent church members' meeting. The elders shall obtain the consent of the nominees, for either office, after which their names shall be published before the church two Lord's days before the election. Elections shall take place at a church meeting duly called for that purpose, and shall be by ballot. A two-thirds majority of those present shall be necessary to secure election. To avoid confusion, election of elders and election of deacons shall not take place at the same time.

G. FINANCE

31. The proclamation of the gospel and the public worship of God entail certain necessary expenses, and each member is lovingly reminded of his or her definite responsibility in this connection, and is asked to study the principles of receiving from and giving to the Lord as set forth in His word, that His work may not be hindered. See 1 Corinthians 16:1-2; 2 Corinthians 8 & 9; Malachi 3:8-10; etc.

[Comments: We do not monitor the givings of the individual members. All givings should be done regularly, cheerfully, privately, and proportionately. Members should consider tithing, i.e. giving at least 10% of their earnings. There may be occasions when other offerings are made. Failure to give as you ought might cause great inconvenience to the pastor, and hinder the work of the gospel.]

32. If considered necessary, an offering for the needy of the church shall be received after the observance of the Lord's Supper.

33. A statement of accounts shall be presented annually by the Treasurer of the church at a church members' meeting, the accounts having been previously audited by two members (one of whom shall be an office-bearer) appointed by the church.

H. GENERAL CLAUSES

34. No alteration, or addition, to these rules shall be made unless decided after one month's notice by a majority of two-thirds of those members present at a meeting specially convened for the purpose. The dissolution of the church shall follow the same procedure.
[Comments: The Constitution is the charter of the church, the official and solemn agreement entered into by the founding members. It spells out the character and objectives of the church, which may not be altered according to anyone's whims, fancies, or opinions. Only the rules, regulations, and procedures may be amended, and even that, under the stringent conditions of this paragraph.]

35. Members in affliction desiring a visit are asked to communicate with the pastor or any other office-bearer without delay. This will ensure that they receive an early visit.

36. Members changing their residence are requested to communicate the fact immediately to the Church Secretary. Great inconveniences often arise through members neglecting to do this.

37. Nobody shall engage in any teaching capacity in connection with the church without the prior approval of the eldership. This rule also applies to members who preach or teach elsewhere.
[Comments: We encourage the exercise of the individual's gifts, as can

be seen in paragraph 13 of this Polity, point No. 7 of the Doctrinal Statement, and also point (c) of the Covenant. However, teaching is a means of wielding spiritual authority which carries with it weighty implications (James 3:1). It is not right for a member to gather a group of other members to teach them without the approval of the elders. This applies to the use of social media such as Whatsapp and Facebook. The incongruency of one who is not a recognised teacher in the church giving Bible teaching regularly to members of the church is obvious. We do not wish to have the situation of "a church within the church" develop. Furthermore, a member who teaches elsewhere, say in another church, will be seen to be a representative of the church whether he likes it or not. The church encourages members to witness actively to non-believers, and to carry out regular Bible studies with them in their homes, with the knowledge of the elders.]

38. A trustee must be a member of the church and there shall be not more than four trustees of the church. A trustee or trustees shall be elected by a membership meeting by a majority of two-thirds of those members present and voting at a meeting specially convened for such purpose. The property of the church (other than cash which shall be under the control of the Treasurer) shall be vested in them to be dealt with by them as the membership from time to time direct by resolution (of which an entry in the Minute Book shall be conclusive evidence). The trustees shall be indemnified against risk and expenses out of the church property. For the purpose of giving effect to such nomination the Church Secretary for the time being is hereby nominated as the person to appoint new trustees of the church within the meaning of Section 40 of the Trustees Act 1949, and shall by deed duly appoint the person or persons so nominated by the membership as the new trustee or trustees of the church and

the provisions of the Trustees Act 1949 shall apply to any such appointment.[2] Any statement of fact in any such Deed of Appointment shall in favour of a person dealing bona fide and for value with the church be conclusive evidence of the fact stated. The trustees shall meet with the office-bearers at least once in a year, before the Annual General Meeting.

39. In the event of the church being dissolved, all funds and possessions remaining after the payment of all due debts shall be equally divided among the missionaries who have been sent out, and are still being supported, by the church. If there are no supported missionaries, the assets shall be donated to a like-minded, Reformed Baptist, church or churches either in this country or overseas.

****

---

[2]The relevant laws regarding the trustees will differ from country to country. It is best to consult a lawyer on this.

COVENANT OF MEMBERS

In covenanting together as members of Damansara Reformed Baptist Church, it is our intention both to uphold and promote the gospel of our Lord Jesus Christ as summarised in our Doctrinal Statement, and solemnly and carefully to apply ourselves to the duties and privileges of membership of Christ's church.

As far as we are able, we will especially endeavour:

(a) To maintain the worship of God in spirit and in truth.

(b) In dependence upon the Holy Spirit, to live a life at all times which will be an example consistent with the faith we profess: with such love, patience and esteem for one another as will prove we are disciples of Jesus Christ, and will be to the spiritual prosperity of one another.

(c) To participate in such meetings for worship, teaching, fellowship, breaking of bread and prayers as the church shall arrange, and to seek to discover and exercise whatever gifts the Lord bestows upon us to the benefit of His church.

(d) To pray for and encourage the officers of the church in the discharge of their duty, and to contribute to the expenses of the church and the support of its pastor according to our means.

(e) To endeavour to avoid all causes and causers of division, and at all times seek to maintain the unity of the Spirit in the bond of peace.

(f) To be discreet over matters discussed during church members' meetings, and not divulge to others those matters that should be kept within the membership of the church.

(g) To abide by such rules as the church shall from time to time
agree will assist the proper ordering of the church's affairs.

****

Other books by the same author:

1 A BASIC CATECHISM OF THE CHRISTIAN FAITH

2 A GARDEN ENCLOSED: A Historical Study And Evaluation Of The Form Of Church Government Practised By The Particular Baptists In The 17th And 18th Centuries.

3 AGAINST PARITY: A Response To The Parity View Of The Church Eldership

4 CESSATIONISM OR CONTINUATIONISM?: An Exposition of 1 Corinthians 12-14 and Related Passages

5 FLEE ALSO YOUTHFUL LUSTS: An Exposition of 2 Timothy 2:22

6 INDEPENDENCY: The Biblical Form Of Church Government

7 SATAN'S STRATEGY, GOD'S REMEDY (evangelistic booklet)

8 TAMING JACOB: How A Restless Soul Found Peace With God

9 THE CHRISTIAN IN THE CHINESE CULTURE

10 THE FUNDAMENTALS OF OUR FAITH: Studies On The 1689 Baptist Confession Of Faith

11 THE HIDDEN LIFE: A Call To Discipleship

12 THE KEYS OF THE KINGDOM: A Study On The Biblical Form Of Church Government

13 THE ROSE OF SHARON, THE LILY OF THE VALLEYS: An Exposition on the Song of Solomon

14 THOROUGHGOING REFORMATION: What It Means To Be Truly Reformed

15 WHAT IS A REFORMED BAPTIST CHURCH?

16 WORLD MISSIONS TODAY: A Theological, Exegetical, and Practical Perspective Of Missions

9 789839 180374